REDEEMING RELEVANCE

IN THE
BOOK OF GENESIS

EXPLORATIONS IN TEXT AND MEANING

מעשה אבות סימן לבנים

REDEEMING RELEVANCE

IN THE
BOOK OF GENESIS

EXPLORATIONS IN TEXT AND MEANING

RABBI FRANCIS NATAF

URIM PUBLICATIONS

David Cardozo Academy

Jerusalem

Redeeming Relevance in the Book of Genesis: Explorations in Text and
Meaning
by Francis Nataf

Urim Publications, P.O. Box 52287, Jerusalem 91521 Israel
Lambda Publishers Inc.
3709 13th Avenue Brooklyn, New York 11218 U.S.A.
Tel: 718-972-5449 Fax: 718-972-6307, mh@ejudaica.com

www.UrimPublications.com

CONTENTS

This book is dedicated to the memory of
Dr. Ludwig Strauss *z"l*
who by sharing
the light and depth of Jewish learning
transformed my life.
His memory blesses his family
and all who came to know him.

Richard Lemon

PREFACE

For thousands of years, Jews have read a portion of the Torah in the synagogue every Shabbat. It is customary to begin the first portion on Simchat Torah and to finish the Torah on the same day a year later. Once the last verses of the book of *Devarim* (Deuteronomy) are read and the Torah scroll is closed, a second scroll is brought and the Torah reader starts all over again with the story of Creation in the book of *Bereshit* (Genesis). This happens within seconds, and there is barely time to breathe between the first and the second readings. It is as if any delay would be dangerous. And indeed it would be. The Torah is the life-blood of the Jewish people, and any hampering of its flow would be detrimental. It is the Jewish people's portable homeland, and for millennia it has been seen and experienced as the Divine voice speaking to all generations, instructing them in the correct way of living.

But why start reading the Torah all over again after merely a year – such a short period of time? Why not read a few verses a week in the synagogue, and dwell on them throughout the week so as to figure them out and truly understand them? Why not take tens of years for one complete cycle and carefully study the Torah's contents piece by piece? After all, what is the difference between the first and the second readings – or between the thousandth and thousandth-and-first readings – when the reading stays superficial? What has been gained?

Human beings grow, change, and constantly transform themselves. And when one brings his experiences to the text, the text gets transformed as well. Human experience itself functions as a kind of commentary on the Biblical text. The dynamic human being depicts himself in the text, and as such the text takes on an entirely new meaning every moment. Consequently, the Biblical text cannot stagnate. What can stagnate man and the Biblical text is man's inability to recognize and explore his own growth and change.

Conversely, the text also changes man. By reading the entire Torah scroll every year and being confronted by the sum total of the text, a person realizes that many of the Biblical stories presented in the Torah are an explanation of his life. But not only that. The truth is that one needs *all* the stories in order to understand one single moment in his life. All of the stories are represented in *this* moment; layers and layers of one's own life-moment are revealed as a kind of *Traumdeutung*. It is for this reason that the Jew is asked to complete the reading of the Torah scroll within a year: He needs to be reminded of the broadness of the text, so as to understand the implication of one narrow moment in his life.

In *Redeeming Relevance,* my dear friend Rabbi Francis Nataf, educational director of the David Cardozo Academy, has brought his life experiences as an educator to the Biblical text. He shows us how the ancient stories are highly relevant to our lives, as well as how the text itself reveals the depth of our lives as individuals and as a people. Moreover, he teaches us how we need to approach some of the most difficult life challenges. In these fine essays, Rabbi Nataf proves that the Torah was passed on to us not as closed, boxed-in wisdom, but as an open-ended, ongoing conversation between its Author and the people of Israel – and through it to all of mankind.

He is to be complimented for his original insights and the eloquence of his language.

We at the David Cardozo Academy are honored to have this book published.

May the Master of the Universe bless him.

Rabbi Nathan Lopes Cardozo, Ph.D.
Dean of the David Cardozo Academy, Jerusalem

Letter from Rabbi Dr. Aharon Lichtenstein

The resurgence of the study of Tanakh in Israel – in dati-leumi Torah circles, in particular – has been justly welcomed as a most positive development. Constituting both an expansion of the horizons of *talmud Torah* and an expression of bonding with the cradle of most of Tanakh within the context of *shivat Zion*, this renascence has unquestionably enriched and enhanced the spiritual life of a revitalized community.

   Unfortunately, however, this enterprise has, at times, been accompanied by negative elements, as well. Perhaps most regrettable has been the tendency on the part of some scholars, students, or observers to constrict the content, scope and significance of much of Tanakh. Familiarity with the text, in one sense, has, in some circles, bred familiarity with the Scriptural narrative and the events and their protagonists presented therein, in another. The sense of reverential awe and the awareness of heroic stature may become jaded and replaced by what is cried up as "eye-level Tanakh study." To be sure, in one respect, the eye-level approach is to be welcomed, insofar as it serves as a healthy antidote to the radical and sweeping idealization and etherealization – and, hence, dehumanization – which characterized some latter-day *parshanut*. Surely, recognition of the human and emotional dimension of even our greatest – so amply, vigorously, and imaginatively portrayed by *midrashim* – is critical for a proper understanding of their lives and their meaning. But when this reactive response to previous excesses goes overboard; when eye-level confrontation is taken to entail not only acknowledgment of overarching humanity but envisions the meeting, shorn of majesty, grandeur, and élan, at the plane of my own very mundane existence; and when, as sometimes occurs, this approach is accompanied by the benign neglect of much of the treasures of traditional *parshanut* and the *midrashim*, to boot – the spiritual loss can be enormous.

Within this context, Rabbi Francis Nataf's *Redeeming Relevance in the Book of Genesis: Explorations in Text and Meaning* constitutes a welcome and worthwhile contribution to the corpus of yeshiva-oriented elucidation of Tanakh. The volume is comprised of a series of independent and yet related essays, each dealing with a significant episode or personage, drawn from *Sefer Bereshit.* Above all, however, in the tradition of the Ramban and the Netziv, Rabbi Nataf fuses reverence for our greatest with awareness of their humanity; moreover, he recognizes that the human element does not compromise the greatness but, rather, ennobles it. I presume that some of his specific interpretations and judgments will draw criticism from the left or from the right; and the overall balance he has struck may likewise invite some variegated challenge. However, the serious and sensitive initiative to cope with the substantive issues as well as with their educational ramifications deserves the respect of a broad range of readers. Rabbi Nataf's fresh voice is one the Torah world will find well worth hearing.

בברכת התורה והמצוה,

Aharon Lichtenstein

ACKNOWLEDGMENTS

This book, *Redeeming Relevance*, is the result of many years of teaching the Biblical text. During these years, I have been developing my own thoughts about some of the central messages conveyed by our holy Torah and how these messages can give us the wisdom with which to live our lives within modern society.

Many people have been involved in the process that began when I first enrolled in yeshiva and ultimately led to the publication of this book. It is not just my own book; *Redeeming Relevance* really belongs to my teachers and students as well. My teachers opened up the rich Jewish tradition to me and gave me the skills to plumb its depths on my own. Although my teachers are too numerous to list, I cannot forgo mentioning Rabbi Aharon Lichtenstein, *shlita*, whose approach and example continue to serve as my guiding light. In the context of my approach to Bible *per se,* I must cite my tutelage under Nechama Leibowitz, *z"l,* who taught me to develop a systematic approach to the Biblical text as well as to appreciate the rabbis' mastery of that text. My many students across the world have been instrumental in the development of my work as well. They have provided me with a sounding board and a forum for developing my ideas together with them. Their enthusiasm for my thoughts and their oft-repeated suggestion that I write these thoughts down and make a book, served as the immediate catalyst for this work.

I have taught Bible at many institutions and for many groups. Still, the bulk of my mature work in Bible has taken place at Midreshet Rachel v'Chaya College of Jewish Studies in Jerusalem. My students there have been invaluable partners in my *Avodat haKodesh.* I am most grateful to its directors, Rabbi Yitzchak Shurin and Mrs. Lynn Finson, for giving me the opportunity to teach in such an open forum as they provide. I thank them and my colleagues there for their support and encouragement.

I am most grateful to my dear friend and colleague, Rabbi Nathan Lopes Cardozo, without whom this book and many other personal projects may have remained dreams. It is in working together with him, in the context of the David Cardozo Academy, that I have been able to truly develop my talents in front of the larger public and to work on issues of great importance to the Jewish people. More than anything else, it is his weighty endorsement of my work that has given it the attention I hope it merits. I thank him for his confidence in me, and for the great honor of working with him over the last few years.

The staff, students, and supporters of the David Cardozo Academy have provided a most receptive home for my thoughts and for my career. Without them, my work would feel like a lone effort. In this context, I want to thank Mrs. Esther Peterman, the Academy's administrative assistant, who has given her best efforts to making sure that every detail is taken care of in an efficient and timely manner. Although this has always been the case, it has been especially apparent in her patient help in matters connected to the publication of this book.

Among our supporters, I count many dedicated friends who have happily given of their time and resources. In particular, the publication of this book is due to the generosity of Mr. Richard Lemon of Napa, California. He seeks to live a life of truth, and humbly encourages those who desire to improve the human condition. It is an honor to know him and to have this book dedicated by him.

Both via the Cardozo Academy and through many publications, websites, and blogspots, my regular column known as *Ideas* has given me the opportunity to reach a varied and receptive readership. I am very grateful to that readership and especially to those who have corresponded with me about my various articles over the last six years since the column's inception.

On the editorial side, I want to thank Sharona Hakimi and the staff at Urim Publications and its director, Tzvi Mauer. Working with Tzvi and Urim is a great pleasure. Moreover, to be counted as an author for Urim means being at the forefront of quality Jewish literature. In particular, I want to thank Tzvi for his encouragement and flexibility – there is not much more one can ask from a publisher. Thanks also go to Rabbi Yonatan Kolatch and especially to Dr. Avivah Gottlieb Zornberg for their review of my manuscript. Mrs. Simi Peters, Rabbi Mois Navon, and Rabbi Avi Silverman provided valuable feedback on Chapter 5, the first one to be written. I also want to thank Rabbi Norman Lamm and Rabbi Saul Berman, who, along with Rav Lichtenstein, agreed to review the manuscript and provide the book with their valuable endorsements.

On a personal note, I want to thank my family. My parents, Fernand and Mireille Nataf, gave me the foundation and lifelong encouragement to accomplish great things. My parents-in-law, Sheldon and Marion Cohen, have always shown concern and support for me and my family. My children, Yoel, Amalia, Tamar, and Sa'adia, daily give us pride and show us more and more that they will be our greatest contribution to the Jewish people in its rebirth on our ancient land.

More than any other person, however, I owe a great debt of gratitude to my wife, Deena. In this case, Rabbi Akiva's words about his own wife, that "both mine and yours are hers," ring true in more ways than one. It is true as Rabbi Akiva meant it – her patience and support have allowed me to seriously pursue my involvement in Torah education and study throughout our married life. But she also has a direct role in most of my writings, including *Redeeming Relevance,* as my primary editor. In this capacity, she has diligently worked to create a far more literate and accessible text. It is my great fortune that she was able to apply her formidable talents to this book. Most important, she has been a wonderful partner in our life's commitment to help bring God's presence to our People and into the world.

Ultimately it is to the Almighty that I must give all my praise and appreciation. The skills that I have acquired and the opportunities that have crossed my life's path are all from Him. My prayer is that I am able to use them to their fullest potential and that my teachings serve to bring both my readers and myself closer to His will.

I offer this book to the general public with great hesitation. I am aware of my shortcomings and relative youth, and constantly remind myself of the example set by the famous Maharal of Prague, whose voluminous works were only written in the later years of his life. Torah wisdom is cumulative and is best expressed by those who have had many decades of experience. Nevertheless, the encouragement from the many people who have expressed their interest in my thoughts even at this stage has given me the impetus to share this work with others.

The essays in this book are the first fruits of the literary contribution I hope to make. Like all first fruits, there will certainly be room for further improvement and refinement. May God allow me to continue to improve and refine my work, and to fathom the depths of His holy Torah.

Francis Nataf
Jerusalem
Tishrei 5767 (2006)

Redeeming Our Torah

The last century has been a most tumultuous one for the Jewish people. The changes in family structure and geographic distribution, as well as the internalization of modernity, have radically transformed the Jews from what they had been before.

Even the Orthodox community, which has attempted to preserve the world of the past, has been greatly affected by this. In that community's writings, change is more evident from what is not being said than from what is being said. The profound and original thinking characteristic of a strong, self-confident culture has largely given way to restatement and reformulation of past writings, something that is associated with a culture under siege. As will be discussed later, this is especially the case when it comes to original thought aimed at interpreting Judaism's most basic source – the Bible.

In this context, the following introduction of a well-respected educator and prominent rabbi's book is most revealing:

> I have avoided citations from Torah literature. I do not feel myself qualified to interpret the words of our sages nor do I feel that I have the right to attempt to use [Talmudic literature] as a means of proving my contentions.
>
> Doing so would have cheapened the words of the Torah and also might have led to adapting [Talmudic literature] to fit

one's personal theory rather than adapting one's theory to fit [Talmudic literature].

No doubt, this rabbi's intentions are praiseworthy. He does not want to cheapen the Torah, nor to risk misinterpreting it. His fears are not unfounded: In recent years, there have certainly been many writers who have suggested superficial or even silly teachings based on their own reading of the Torah. Such interpretations certainly have diminished the words of the Torah and its classical commentaries.

Even though his fears are well founded, the alternative implicitly suggested may be even worse. If a leading Jewish educator can write a major essay without referring back to our classical sources, what does this say about the impact of the Torah in our times? If we do not even attempt to check our ideas against the Torah and its accompanying literature, where does that leave the supposed centrality of Torah in our lives, the lives of today's Jews? Are we to study our classical texts only as an intellectual exercise? *Out of fear of misreading our holy texts then, we are relegating them to irrelevance.* Regardless of whether or not this was the intention of the rabbi quoted above, we see fewer and fewer attempts to seek the Torah's guidance regarding new ideas and behavior that are emerging in all sectors of the Jewish community.

This is the way one treats antiquities: by protecting them in museums, the artifacts lose any relevance to the present. In contrast, this is not the way Jews have treated their Torah throughout history. From time immemorial, Jews have taken the risk of misinterpreting the Torah. They have done so in order to find guidance, inspiration, and truth for themselves and their communities. This, perhaps more than anything else, has allowed our ancient Torah to be a living document for the Jewish people.

It is no accident, then, that so many Torah commentators have recorded ideas based on the Torah and its accompanying literature that spoke to these commentators' cultural realities. From Ramban's discussion of persecutions, to Abarbanel's treatment of statesmanship, to Rabbi Samson Raphael Hirsch's insights on freedom and the dignity of man, readers in their respective periods were surely grateful to find their own concerns addressed by authentic readings of the Torah.

Indeed, many who have discarded the Torah in modern times have done so out of a sense that it addresses exclusively the worldview of the ancients and not that of people today. The Torah's perceived irrelevance has caused people to lose interest in it and in Judaism altogether. Consequently, seeking the Torah's relevance for our times is of major practical consequence.

This book starts with the need to return to the profound originality, characteristic of Jewish tradition, in interpreting our classical texts. In this we would do well to take our guidance from the greats of yesteryear who, as in most things, show us the true ways of our rich tradition.

In order to return to the creativity of the past, we will first need to discuss its underlying assumptions.

Multiplicity of Meaning

It is certainly true that a text will generally be most relevant to the geographical and historical culture in which it was written. The nature of what we refer to as a classic work, however, is that it contains many elements, the relevance of which transcends its own culture. Still, the greater the disparity between the respective cultures of the writer on the one hand and the reader on the other, the more unlikely that even a classic work can truly be relevant to the reader. This issue is an important consideration in elucidating the Torah's relevance hundreds and thousands of years after its writing. Here, the disparity is not between author and reader but between the original intended audience and subsequent readers. After all, it would be like sticking our heads in the sand to pretend that we have the same exact material culture, beliefs and attitudes as Jews did in all previous time periods. As a result, some scholars would tell us that seeking relevance in the Torah is quite artificial, since the intention of the text was to convey information to a specific historical culture, one far removed from our own. While such scholars would not deny the relevance of certain universal ideas that exist in the Torah, they would contend that the Torah's relevance is really quite limited.

Throughout history, however, Jews have understood the Torah to be a document that was meant for every generation.[1] This, presumably without the help of contemporary academic trends in literary analysis and critique which deemphasize the *intended* meaning of texts. While such trends may indeed have some parallels in classical Jewish sources, it is highly unlikely that Jewish Biblical exegetes rooted their search for relevance in such thought.[2] Rather, the classical search for relevance seems to be rooted in what commentators perceived to be the unique properties that emanate from the Torah's Divine authorship. That is to say, whereas a human author's meaning is necessarily limited by his culture, God's intentions and meaning can span whatever possibilities the words can legitimately carry.[3] God's ability to communicate two contradictory things at once is actually illustrated in a different context by

---

[1] See Nechama Leibowitz, "A Torah for All Seasons and Persons," in *Studies in Devarim* (Jerusalem: World Zionist Organization, 1963) pp. 50–55.

[2] See R. Aharon Lichtenstein, "Torat Hesed and Torat Emet," in *Leaves of Faith* (Jersey City, NJ: Ktav, 2003) especially pp. 80–82, for an interesting treatment of similarities and differences between various contemporary trends in literary criticism and the freedom of interpretation common in post-rabbinic literature.

[3] It is interesting to note that the famous literary scholar and critic, E.D. Hirsch, half-jokingly concedes that the limits on meaning engendered by an author's culturally determined intentions only apply to a human author and not to a Divine one. See E.D. Hirsch, *Validity in Interpretation* (New Haven: Yale University Press, 1967) p. 126, note 37.

a famous midrash. In the *Mechilta*, we read that when delivering the Decalogue (specifically, the fourth commandment), God said two different words, *shamor* and *zachor,* at the same time.[4] What is illustrated here about God's ability to communicate two *words* simultaneously – which the Midrash points out is impossible for a human speaker – can provide a paradigm for God's propensity to communicate simultaneous *meanings* of the words actually written in the Torah.

In his classic work, *Duties of the Heart (Chovot haLevavot)*, R. Bachya ibn Pakuda addresses this very point. Regarding the Torah's use of physical human imagery to describe God, R. Bachya writes:

Had Scripture [not used anthropomorphisms], the majority of mankind… would have been left without a religion. But the word which may be understood in a material sense will not hurt the intelligent person, since he recognizes its real meaning. And it will help the simple, as its use will result in fixing in his heart and mind the conception that he has a Creator Whom he is bound to serve.[5]

In other words, God expressly used human imagery to describe Himself, *wanting* simple people to read such imagery on a literal level and more sophisticated people to read it on a figurative level.

An even clearer, though more localized example of this idea is found in the words of Don Yitzchak Abarbanel, who explains how God set up Avraham to misunderstand that which He was saying:

In order that Avraham not know [God's] true intention [not to have Yitzchak sacrificed], He spoke to him words that can be

---

[4] *Mechilta*, Chap. 87.

[5] R. Bachya ibn Pakuda, *Duties of the Heart,* Trans. Moses Hyamson (Jerusalem: Feldheim Publishers, 1962), Sha'ar haYichud (Vol. 1) Chap. 10.

understood in two different ways (*devarim sovlim shnei perushim*). Avraham would understand one of them and God would mean the other.[6]

Here we see the use of a phrase which, according to Abarbanel, was expressly used in order that it would be understood in contradictory ways.

The two examples cited above clearly show how major classical commentators understood that God intentionally seeks to convey more than one message through the words of the Torah, whenever needed. This gives the Torah the critical capacity mentioned earlier – to communicate several meanings simultaneously.

In a similar vein, our sages teach us that there are different but equally valid modes for understanding the words of the Torah. In this case, we are not speaking of multiple simultaneous meanings but rather of multiple approaches to the derivation of meaning. Still, it is helpful in understanding how Jewish tradition allowed for a pluralistic approach to the text. For example, the rabbis spent a great deal of time trying to understand the text via various technical patterns (*derash*) which went beyond the literal meaning and sometimes even contradicted it, as in the famous verse that speaks about repaying an "eye for an eye."[7] In doing so, they did not dismiss the plain meaning (*peshat*) – they simply claimed that it was less relevant in certain cases. While one mode of understanding may be more relevant for any given statement, both modes remain true. Any scholar who would have refused to entertain any *derash* because it was contrary to common sense would have been thrown out of the Talmudic academy. Similarly, anyone who would have rejected *peshat*

---

[6] Abarbanel, *Bereshit* 22:11–12.

[7] *Shemot* 21:24. The Rabbis interpret this verse to mean that the perpetrator of the crime must pay the monetary value of the victim's eye (*Baba Kama* 84a).

automatically because of its "childish" simplicity would have likewise lost his academic standing.

It is thus likely that multiplicity of intended meaning was assumed by almost all the classical commentators, who found insights in the Torah that could not have been understood at the time of its writing. This is indeed the sense of the phrase made famous by Ramban: *Ma'aseh Avot Siman leBanim*, i.e., the actions of the forefathers would relate to events that would happen much later. What was understood as simple narrative by the fathers would actually contain useful advice to their descendants later on.[8]

The traditional assumption of multiple meanings in the Torah allowed Jewish commentators throughout the generations to find meaning inaccessible to previous generations. This approach maintains that the meaning was always there, but one has to have the right colored glasses to notice a particular message. To quote a thoughtful acquaintance, "A blind man can never recognize the appeal of a sunset"; in other words, all mortals are blind to what is beyond their ability to perceive. As such, all men are limited in what they recognize as real and true. Patterns, words, and relationships are all interpreted from where we stand in time and place (i.e., our cultural context). Each generation's cultural context brought about understandings that could not have been noticed by those who had come before.[9] Indeed, it would make sense that the intended

---

[8] See Nechama Leibowitz, *Studies in Bereshit* (Jerusalem: World Zionist Organization, 1963) pp. 369–70 (*Vayishlach* 4), and Rut Ben Meir in *Pirkei Nechama* (Jerusalem: Jewish Agency, 2001) pp. 137–38.

[9] An important corollary is that later generations are able to revive old, relatively ignored observations whose relevance was lost on many intervening generations, until the cultural context once more fits the ancient observation. That is to say, history does repeat itself. Certain ideas or attitudes lose their popularity, only to resurface later in history. Indeed, the Renaissance was a period in general history where many notions of classical Greece and Rome were rediscovered. Likewise, the multifaceted views found in Talmudic literature have very commonly been reviewed and revived by later commentators in such a fashion.

timelessness of the Torah would factor its readers' cultural, historical and personal subjectivity into the text. Thus, it is a tribute to the Torah's Divine nature that its richness of meaning has allowed for so many insights and understandings to be discovered by one generation after another.

There are many examples of changing cultural attitudes and assumptions that require different understandings in different time periods. For our purposes we will suffice with two well-known examples:

The earth's age. The Torah somehow has to communicate the age of the earth to the ancients, whose numerical and scientific orientation was totally different from modern man's. At the same time, however, Torah's timelessness requires it to leave clues as to the vast amounts of time that actually elapsed during the earth's creation to be discovered in the text by modern man.[10]

Physiological references to God. It is well-known that R. Avraham ben David (Ravad) took Rambam to task for making the incorporeality of God an essential condition of Jewish faith.[11] Ravad claims that many great Jews did not share this belief with Rambam. If Ravad is correct, this could be another example of the Torah's need to camouflage truth from generations not yet prepared to understand it. That is to say, ancient Jews may have needed to understand God in anthropomorphic terms.

In both of these examples, the Torah needs to express contradictory details of the story to suit its different historical readerships. While one meaning may be truer to reality than the other, both are intended, and therefore valid, meanings.

In summary, it appears that a major implicit assumption underlying the traditional search for original insights is that the words and narratives of the Torah were often intended to mean different things to

---

[10] See Nathan Aviezer, *In the Beginning* (Hoboken, NJ: Ktav, 1990) pp. 1–5, and Nosson Slifkin, *The Science of Torah* (Jerusalem: Targum, 2001) pp. 100–34.

[11] *Mishneh Torah,* Hilchot Teshuva 3:7.

different cultures. The Torah's need to be relevant to all generations requires that it express different things to different people with the same words.

The Pursuit of Relevance in Modern Times

This book attempts to be unusual, aiming to interpret the Bible in new ways. While informed of and influenced by normative Jewish and rabbinic tradition, I have consciously chosen to seek novel understandings of the text. Yet even if this is uncommon in our days, it is certainly not a departure from Jewish tradition.

When Modernity first encountered traditional Judaism, and especially in the nineteenth century, there were many Jewish thinkers who sought Torah-driven answers to the myriad issues posed by the new ways in which man looked at his world. In this regard, Rabbi Samson Raphael Hirsch was possibly the most successful at reaping textually rooted insights for the modern Jew. Hirsch was likely motivated by the need to win over the loyalty of ambivalent German Jews to the Divine authority of the Torah. Many other great Western European rabbis were also involved in similar efforts to show the Torah's timelessness to their constituents. Among the most famous are Rabbis Shmuel David Luzzatto of Italy, Tzvi David Hoffmann of Germany and Joseph H. Hertz of England. But it was not only in Western Europe that recent Jewish scholars strove to find contemporary relevance for the Biblical text. This also occurred in the Eastern European strongholds of Talmudic scholarship. Such greats as Rabbis Baruch haLevi Epstein[12] and Naftali Tzvi Yehudah Berlin,[13] both Lithuanians, also elucidated the Biblical text, very much with an eye to the modern world around them.

---

[12] *Torah Temimah.*

[13] *Ha'amek Davar.*

It is worth noting that compared to the nineteenth century, the twentieth century did not produce many great commentaries of relevance. While some may disagree with such a bold statement, all one need do is look at the commentaries that sit on the shelves of most yeshivot and traditional homes. One will likely find many works from the nineteenth century but very little from the twentieth century. Instead, the few great voices who devoted serious work to *parshanut* (traditional commentary) in the last hundred years focused on technical scholarship, either of the academic type (i.e., Umberto Cassuto) or of the Talmudic type (i.e., Rabbi Meir Simcha of Dvinsk, author of *Meshech Chochma*[14]). It is not within the scope of this Introduction to elaborate on the many reasons for these developments in *parshanut*. More important to us is to identify this trend as deviant in Jewish history and to seek ways to return to the traditional Jewish path of seeking relevance.

An obstacle on the road back to relevance is the flightiness of Biblical sermonics both within and outside of Orthodoxy. As people have always intuitively sought relevance, the vacuum in serious relevant commentaries has forced the hands of pulpit rabbis, novelists and celebrities to fill the gap. Indeed, such writers sometimes have found important insights.[15] Still, without proper background and training, the most intelligent writer cannot be expected to come out with a consistently serious work.[16] The resultant childish and amateur nature of much that proclaims itself to be relevant has given "relevance" a bad name.

---

[14] Although published in the last century, it was actually written in the nineteenth century in his youth.

[15] In my own teaching experience, I have often been amazed by the profound insights of students who often do not have extensive backgrounds in the field.

[16] See, for example, Alan Dershowitz's *The Genesis of Justice* (New York: Warner Books, 2000) for an example of a brilliant writer whose analysis of the Biblical text leaves much to be desired.

In the twentieth century, then, we found ourselves with scholarship on one side and relevance on the other, a bifurcation foreign to traditional Jewish commentary which, precisely to the contrary, has usually sought to present something scholarly yet accessible to the average Jew. With an appreciation of the average Jew's need to find relevance in the text, serious Jewish scholars have historically used their talents and expertise to find a contemporary reading of the text. It is my intention in this volume to show that this can be done in our own time as well. In *Redeeming Relevance*, I discuss six different themes, in the order of their appearance in the Biblical text. In choosing these themes, I have sought out patterns that carry important implications for the serious contemporary Jew.

The classical Jewish commentaries serve as our model. While we may not be able to claim the intelligence or scholarship of these luminaries, we can try to emulate the seriousness of their approach to the text. This means that, first and foremost, we must try to understand the text according to its various modes, and only *then* look for relevance as it emerges naturally from our study. When we allow the Torah to speak, we will find that, as in all generations, it does, in fact, speak *to us*. We must, however, allow the Torah to speak in *its* fashion, through its allusions, patterns, nuances, associations, and intentional ambiguities. This is not to deny the legitimate subjectivity of the commentator as previously mentioned. Rather, it is to say that a commentator cannot purposely impose his own preconceptions onto the text.[17]

The chapters in this book represent my modest attempt to start the ball rolling. As mentioned in the Acknowledgments, I have mixed feelings about presenting my thoughts to a larger audience. Nonetheless, hundreds of my students, readers and colleagues have felt that the ideas included in these pages are relevant and rigorous. If they are correct, I

---

[17] This idea is discussed at greater length in the Afterword.

view it as my obligation to show more people the types of insights that can and should be gleaned from God's sacred and beautiful Torah.

Still, I am only too aware that my attempts at rigor and relevance are limited by time, ability and erudition. By offering these essays to the public, I am not pretending that they are flawless. Moreover, the danger inherent in the pursuit of relevance is to read things into the text that are not really there, in spite of one's most sincere efforts not to do so. As such, rather than presenting the essays as authoritative, I humbly ask the reader to view them as an invitation to dialogue. Perhaps, as with all Jewish learning, creating such a dialogue will allow us to truly develop the best relevant insights, which is, in fact, the ultimate purpose of this book.

More than the content, however, I hope that readers will appreciate the approach manifest in these essays. My approach is based on the conviction that we must work carefully and creatively to find the Torah's intended meaning for our time. An appreciation of the approach and that which is behind it will not only encourage this writer, but will go a long away toward **redeeming relevance**.

CHAPTER 1

Redeeming Our Souls: Avraham's Ninth Test

Biblical Heroes

We are not always sure what to think of our Biblical ancestors. Sometimes their feats appear superhuman, and at other times their mistakes are too painfully clear. For the inexperienced student, this creates a certain cognitive dissonance, which may lead to hasty and forced interpretations aimed at creating more homogeneous characters. As a student becomes more experienced and sophisticated, he will likely become more comfortable with this lack of uniformity, realizing that rather than a weakness, the Torah's nuanced portrayal of our ancestors is quite true to real life. Thus, if the Torah is trying to teach us about the lives of real people, we should not expect to read about artificially one-dimensional characters, as this is not the nature of actual men and women. While appropriately sophisticated, this realistic complexity still creates some confusion as we attempt to find a proper perspective on the Torah's great figures.

Indeed, maintaining an appropriate perspective of our Biblical heroes is one of the most serious issues that a Jewish Educator must face. Making them too great or not great enough is as pernicious as it is common. The cost of misunderstanding our heroes' actions and thinking of them as "just like everyone else" is clear to most religious Jews. Without the needed reverence and awe for them, they lose their power as the effective role models that they have been from time immemorial. Consequently, most traditional commentators carefully examine actions that seem incongruent with a certain character's standing, seeking to find more subtle explanations than what would appear from a superficial reading.

What many teachers and students do not realize, however, is that the other side of this equation is equally problematic. When we make our heroes into angels who operate without the difficulties inherent in natural human existence, we also prevent them from being true role models. This is because we can only hold ourselves accountable to that which has been accomplished by real people who faced the same sort of challenges as we do.[1] This too was understood by the vast majority of traditional commentators, who start with the premise that our heroes are fallible and therefore not beyond criticism – even as that criticism must be very sober and respectful.

It is within this context of natural human existence that we need to study the various tests encountered by Avraham in the Torah. In our attempt to grasp the relevance of his tests for us, we must remember that Avraham was a spiritual giant. Yet it is critical that we also note that he was not born that way. In other words, Avraham was not a static individual. He is not the exact same person when he is first told to move to Eretz Yisrael as he is much later, when God asks him to kill his son Yitzchak. He has developed in a way that is natural and, therefore, instructive. Indeed, from the point of view of natural human development, the well-known rabbinic tradition that Avraham encountered ten different trials[2] takes on a significance that may otherwise be overlooked. Rather than seeing these tests as independent of one another, as would be the case with ten distinct missions given to ten

---

[1] See the famous comments of Rabbi S.R. Hirsch on *Bereshit* 12:10.

[2] *Avot* 5:3.

different people, we can understand the ten trials as one singular path outlining Avraham's moral and spiritual development.

We must now carefully look at the text itself to see how the Torah helps us understand Avraham's pattern of growth. Comparing the tradition of Avraham's many tests to the Biblical text[3] leads us to a question: If, as the rabbis claim, the ten different challenges faced by Avraham are all to be viewed as trials, why then does the text explicitly describe only his last ordeal,[4] when he is called to sacrifice Yitzchak, as a trial? Should not the Torah have described all ten incidents as trials?

The more one studies the binding of Yitzchak, however, the more one appreciates the Torah's creating a special category for this one particular test.[5] In fact, it is so unique that it is the only place in the entire Torah where the word *nisa* (tested[6]) appears with reference to an individual. While it is almost self-evident that every major decision in Avraham's life had ramifications for his descendants, more than anything else it is his final test that truly established Avraham's legacy. The rabbis make this point in explaining that had Avraham failed the last test, it would have put all of his other accomplishments into question.[7] Of course, once we recognize the critical weight of the last test, we come to ask the opposite question: what was the need for all the other trials; if everything depends on the final test, why bother with the other ones at all?

---

[3] Some commentators have suggested that not all of the tests are actually to be found in the text altogether. Nevertheless, all agree that at least most of the tests relate to events that are recorded in the Torah.

[4] In understanding this to be the last test, we are following the opinion of Rambam. Others present different orders.

[5] See Chapter 2, pp. 43–45 ("Choosing Sarah's Death"), for a more complete discussion of the difficulty of this test.

[6] The word *nisa* is translated here according to the vast majority of commentators. It is worth noting, however, that Rashbam translates the word to mean attack.

[7] *Sanhedrin* 89b.

Sacrificing Yishmael, Sacrificing Yitzchak

Sarah saw the son of Hagar the Egyptian, whom she bore to Avraham, laughing. She said to Avraham, "Expel this maidservant and her son, because the son of this maidservant will not inherit with my son, with Yitzchak." This [matter] was very evil in the eyes of Avraham, on account of his son. God said to Avraham, "Don't let it be evil in your eyes concerning the boy and concerning your maidservant – everything that Sarah tells you, listen to her voice…. And also the son of the maidservant I will make into a nation since he is your seed." Avraham got up early in the morning... and he sent her away. (*Bereshit* 21:9–14)

God tested Avraham, and He said to him, "Avraham." [Avraham] said, "Here I am." He said, "Please take your son, your only one, whom you love, Yitzchak, and go to the land of Moriah and bring him up as a sacrifice on one of the mountains that I will tell you." Avraham got up early in the morning and he saddled his donkey and he took... Yitzchak his son. (*Bereshit* 22:1–3)

In order to understand the need for Avraham's first nine tests, it is worthwhile to focus our attention on what may be the most revealing of these earlier tests – the expulsion of Avraham's first son, Yishmael. Rambam enumerates this as the penultimate test.[8] This test almost immediately precedes and somehow sets the stage for Avraham's final ordeal with his other son, Yitzchak.

Even without its role as a trial for Avraham, the expulsion of Yishmael is among the most difficult stories in the Torah to understand. The Torah does not explicitly tell us how Yishmael's behavior prompted

---

[8] *Commentary on the Mishna – Avot* 5:3, possibly based on *Yalkut Shimoni*, Parashat Vayera 94, which also identifies this as the ninth trial.

Sarah to ask Avraham for his expulsion. Since her demand follows her observation of Yishmael laughing (or playing), we can surmise that there was something negative about this behavior. Still, it is difficult to read into Yishmael's laughter something that could have warranted her extreme reaction.

The severity of Yishmael's expulsion is underscored by the harsh manner in which he is sent out and by the fact that he almost dies along the journey. Short of resorting to midrashic explanations that are most likely allegorical,[9] it is hard to justify Sarah's response to Yishmael's behavior. Indeed, Rabbi Shimon bar Yochai objected to such explanations in this context, pointing out the extreme unlikelihood of serious misbehavior by someone under the direct influence of Avraham, who is notably one of the most charismatic individuals presented in the Torah.[10] R. Avraham ibn Ezra goes even further by telling us that Yishmael actually did nothing at all to deserve being sent away. Rather, ibn Ezra posits, he was just acting his age – which reminded Sarah that this son of Hagar was older than her own son Yitzchak and therefore a threat to his inheritance.[11] Yet even without such a suggestion, it is easy to understand Avraham's strong disagreement with Sarah's request to expel Yishmael. Moreover, it would follow that Avraham had every reason to believe that God would back him up in his disagreement. What

---

[9] This is the approach of Rashi, who equates laughing with all types of grievous sins. Yet even Rashi displays his ambivalence about this position a few verses later, pointing out that such a caricature of Yishmael does not really fit in with the simple reading of the text.

[10] *Tosefta, Sota* 6:3.

[11] See also Seforno and Ramban, who also feel that the expulsion is mostly due to competition for Avraham's inheritance. While they understand Yishmael's laughter as directed at Yitzchak, it still does not seem to justify Sarah's response.

is much harder to understand, then, is the fact that God sides with Sarah, telling Avraham to listen to her.[12]

The solution to our problem may actually lie in abandoning the search for a justification for Yishmael's expulsion. This becomes possible when we look at the story within the context of the larger picture of Avraham's trials and specifically in comparison with Avraham's final trial. Without such a perspective, we may miss the remarkable parallels between these two stories. In fact, once we shift our attention, we notice that the core narratives of both stories are almost identical: God asks Avraham to do away with his son, knowing the personal anguish this will cause him and yet still expecting Avraham to put his own beliefs and preferences aside – which Avraham faithfully does in carrying out his mission.[13]

Indeed, if we see Yishmael's expulsion as a test of faith for Avraham, certain things become much clearer: Our search for justification is tempered with the realization that God purposefully hid His reasons for this demand. Indeed, had God explained His reasoning to Avraham, the whole test would have been moot. In other words, even though God may have foreseen that Yishmael's expulsion was ultimately

---

[12] This is especially difficult to understand according to Ramban and those who follow his approach of criticizing Sarah for her earlier harsh treatment of Yishmael's mother Hagar (*Bereshit* 16:6). It would seem that Yishmael had done much less than Hagar to deserve such a punishment. While some commentators suggest other answers to this problem (see, for example, R. Chaim Chavel's supercommentary on Ramban regarding this point), it may well be that this very contrast is meant to tempt Avraham to question God, in the same way as the dissonance between God's request that he sacrifice Yitzchak and His promise that Yitzchak will continue Avraham's lineage was set up as a Divine test (see *Bereshit Rabba* 56:8).

[13] Robert Alter has also noticed this pattern. See *The Art of Biblical Narrative* (New York: Basic Books, 1981) pp. 181–82, and *Genesis* (New York: W.W. Norton and Co., 1996) pp. 99, 106.

in everyone's interest,[14] He wanted Avraham to accept it completely on faith.

This was a perfect way to prepare Avraham for his final test with Yitzchak: Just as in the later test, here too God tells Avraham to act against what he thought to be Divine justice and love. As with the binding of Yitzchak, Avraham is tested where he was most vulnerable – the same man who passionately pleaded for strangers in Sodom is told to ignore his powerful trait of loving-kindness when it comes to his own son. In heroic fashion, however, Avraham shows his willingness to completely subordinate himself to the will of God. When he hears the directive concerning Yishmael – as when he hears the decree about Yitzchak – Avraham is essentially asked to sacrifice everything. More than divesting himself of his sons, he is really being asked to divest himself of everything he has become. Avraham built his life around bringing ethical monotheism to the world. Both the content and the future of his efforts would have been undermined by the acts he was now expected to perform. Thus, in these tests, Avraham must place his intellect, his emotions and his entire being on the altar.

If the above parallels are not clear enough, Avraham's response in both cases is expressed with the same exact phrase of *Vayashkem Avraham baboker* ("Avraham got up early in the morning"), a phrase which according to Rashi indicates a person's eagerness to do something.[15] In other words, in both cases Avraham responds to the chilling test with almost superhuman eagerness to do God's bidding.

---

[14] As we shall see in Chapter 3, the rabbis understand that Yishmael mended his ways and later became a righteous man. Although we could say that this occurred in spite of his treatment by Avraham, the comparison with Yitzchak's indulgence of Esav suggests that the policy of "tough love" actually had a positive impact on Yishmael's spiritual growth.

[15] Rashi, *Bereshit* 22:3.

The Need for Process

Now that we have shown the similarity between Avraham's two final tests, we should inquire about the point of this dress rehearsal with Yishmael. Isn't it enough that God tested Avraham with one son? The answer may be that God knew that without the dress rehearsal with Yishmael, Avraham would not have been able to pass his all-important final test with Yitzchak.

Thus, Avraham's trial with Yishmael is intentionally easier than his ultimate test in a number of ways. Most obvious is that he was not asked to kill Yishmael, only to send him away (even though Yishmael almost dies as a result, were it not for Divine intervention). Secondly, it is clear throughout the text that Yitzchak was more precious to Avraham than was Yishmael. Thirdly, as the demand originally came from Sarah, Avraham was able to formulate an independent position before he had to accede to the Divine endorsement of Sarah's request. Finally and perhaps most significantly, God responds to Avraham's feelings for Yishmael and consoles him, telling him that Yishmael will flourish even after his expulsion.

In this way, the Biblical narratives show us a close-up of how one specific religious and emotional challenge prepares Avraham for the next. The main issues that Avraham has to deal with in these two tests are basically the same – namely, the need to put his faith in God even when it requires obedience to a seemingly irrational and unethical demand with devastating personal consequences. However, as opposed to the total surrender required with the sacrifice of Yitzchak, the demand to sacrifice Yishmael comes in a softer, more compromising fashion. On some level, the first test almost suggests the possibility of the other – if God can ask Avraham to put aside his intellect as well as his emotions to get rid of his first son, it is not such a long stretch to think that he could do the same, albeit in much harsher fashion, with the second. One wonders if Avraham had maybe even anticipated the final test, as a result of God's command to expel Yishmael. He might have said to himself, "There could be only one thing harder than what God is asking of me now...."

Our analysis of Avraham's two final tests can also give us insight into the need for the other eight tests. If God felt it necessary for Avraham to go through a dress rehearsal with Yishmael before he could pass his epic final test, the only natural way for him to pass even this penultimate test would be for God to prepare him with graduated tests, each of which would prepare Avraham for the next. In order for a man to master his challenges, he needs suitable preparation. When someone prepares for a great physical feat such as running a marathon, he must build up his physical stamina one step at a time, running progressively longer distances at each stage. The same is true in the spiritual arena: Emotional stamina will only be built by progressively more difficult spiritual challenges.

Although some of the tests are not clearly elucidated, starting with what appears to be the first test – when God tells Avraham to leave his homeland – each test gets progressively more difficult. For example, the first test is coupled with Divine promises assuring Avraham that he has nothing to worry about and that he will only benefit from complying with God's wishes.[16] Such assurances are given to Avraham even though this is a relatively easy request, especially compared to the final two. Still, God's first explicit command needed to be one that Avraham could obey with minimum discomfort, thereby building his confidence for the tests that would follow.

Among some of Avraham's major subsequent tests in order of their appearance are his journey to Egypt to escape famine[17] and Sarah's abduction, first in Egypt[18] and then in Eretz Yisrael.[19] The former is

---

[16] *Bereshit* 12:1–3.

[17] Ibid., 12:10.

[18] Ibid., 12:14–15.

[19] Ibid., 20:2.

something that Avraham may well have accepted as an unavoidable challenge due to the fluctuating weather patterns of the arid Middle East. Moreover, he had recently completed his earlier move from Charan, so emigration was not totally new to him. This was a greater trial than leaving Charan because this time he received no Divine guidance. In fact, God's promise regarding his possession of Eretz Yisrael made it more difficult for Avraham to know how to react to a famine that seemed to compromise his hold on the land.

The next test, the abduction of Sarah, was certainly an even greater test of Avraham's faith in the Divine promises granted him. Now, not only was he stripped of his land, he was also stripped of his wife, who was supposed to bear him the next link in the nascent Jewish people. For Avraham to be a stranger without a land was not completely new. At the same time, whether in Eretz Yisrael or in Egypt, his being a stranger only served to underscore the existential importance of his relationship with Sarah. As a result, the prospect of a life without Sarah was even more difficult for him than the prospect of a life in exile.

Thus, the rest of Avraham's trials follow the same pattern we have established between the ninth and tenth tests. Each one is there to prepare the ground for the next one. In this way, these tests are exactly what allowed Avraham to *become* Avraham.

* * *

The above analysis is especially resonant in modern times, as there is a greater appreciation of human development. Still, even though we are more aware of the gradual way in which people develop, our fast-paced society all too frequently tempts us to take shortcuts in climbing the ladder of success, be it in our careers, our spiritual lives or any other realm. Rabbi J. B. Soloveitchik once pointed out that there can be no holiness without preparation. On a halachic level, this means that anyone who would want to enter the holy areas of the Temple Mount would need to attend to various preparatory matters first. Of course, this notion is meant as more than a halachic insight – we are to understand that the requirement for preparation is part of holiness' intrinsic definition. Like any other accomplishment, holiness cannot come about just by willing it.

It is for this reason that many programs for *ba'alei teshuva* (returnees to traditional Judaism) advise their students to go slowly and to take on mitzvot gradually. It is somewhat of a paradox for Orthodox teachers to advise their students not to take on a fully observant lifestyle – they know that the law is the same for new initiates as for veterans. What such advisers have noticed, however, is that *ba'alei teshuva* are much more likely to stay with observance if they progress slowly. In view of our discussion of Avraham, this makes perfect sense. While in theory one should rigorously observe the mitzvot as soon as one is aware of them, in practice this is not really possible. Like Avraham, we all need to build our observance and cannot ignore the need for process.

Even for those born into religious families, observance is meant to be a process. We must not forget that children are not commanded in mitzvot until they reach the age of twelve or thirteen. The process of preparing the child for this level of observance is what *chinuch*, Jewish education, is all about. In turn, building on this basic level of observance is at the center of a serious Jewish life.

The Biblical narrative of Avraham's life helps us internalize that there can be no shortcuts. Greatness is achieved one step at a time. Great men and women are not born that way – they must successfully pass the small challenges that one by one allow them to reach higher and higher. Were they somehow to bypass all these graduated steps, considering them insignificant, they would never be able to confront the great challenges, which ultimately can be faced only by those with suitable preparation.[20]

---

[20] We can gain a related insight by noting that we read the story of Yishmael's expulsion on the first day of Rosh Hashana, immediately preceding the much more famous second day reading of the binding of Yitzchak. For most of us, the first

We are now in a better position to appreciate the real-life description the Torah gives us of Avraham's life. As it does with other great figures, the Torah creates a model that we can realistically emulate. By showing us Avraham's spiritual development, we can pattern ourselves after him not only in view of his accomplishments, but also with the understanding of how he came to them.

As for the confusion created by normal life-like description of our Biblical heroes discussed at the beginning of this chapter, we need to realize that the Torah can only impart its crucial lessons through a heterogeneous portrayal of our Biblical heroes. The confusion thereby caused is the price we must be willing to pay for the beautiful and sustaining lessons offered to us by this Book of Life.

---

day's reading fails to inspire us in a way appropriate for the most important day of the year. Yet the message may well be that, as with all great human accomplishments, the spiritual renewal of this holiday season cannot happen in a vacuum. On the one hand, if we have failed to properly prepare for Rosh Hashana until we read about the story of Avraham and Yishmael, it should shake us to our very foundations, as we realize that even Avraham could not have passed his final test without serious preparation. On the other hand, another message of the first day's Torah reading is that there is still time for preparation – we should at least use the first day as a dress rehearsal for the second. A dress rehearsal is easier than the actual performance, and we may not be ready for complete *teshuva* on the first day. We should perhaps only aim at a partial *teshuva* on the first day and keep on going from there.

CHAPTER 2

Redeeming Ourselves:
Lessons from the Mothers

The Inevitability of Choice

Democratic society allows for many choices; some highly important, some quite trivial. Today, we choose our careers, our spouses, our homes and many other important facets of our lives. These choices, which we take for granted, were often unavailable in pre-democratic societies.

Yet even as choice is a very central value of Western democracy, the myth known as "the American Dream" tells us that, although we have to make choices within each major source of satisfaction – career, family, wealth and peace of mind – we do not have to choose *between* them. As we grow older, however, most of us eventually see that such a dream is not only elusive, it is impossible. Sooner or later, we all must make choices in our lives, wherein we have to make real and meaningful sacrifices in order to attain what is of greatest importance to us individually.

It could be that previous generations understood this more intuitively. Scarcity of resources and opportunity made it clear to everyone that one could not "have it all." In our times, however, we seem to be less comfortable with trade-offs, being surprised by how much we are unable to attain simply as a result of the human condition.

Even God Can't Have It All

Perhaps we can derive solace when we realize that when acting within the finite, rational world, even God Himself has to make trade-offs. As will be demonstrated, the Biblical text makes this quite clear. (This, of course, is not meant to be a reflection on God, but a reflection on the nature of the world.)

In *Bereshit* 1:26, we have one of the most problematic passages in the entire Torah. To fully grasp the problematic nature of this passage, we must remember that much of Jewish history has been dedicated to fighting against polytheism. It is in this context that we need to understand God's famous statement, "Let *Us* [!?!] make man." While various commentators suggest a variety of reasons why God speaks in the plural,[1] the rabbis[2] acknowledge that this passage will lead to theological errors. Yet these same rabbis explain that it was still worthwhile for God to use this phrase.

The rabbis suggest that God did, in fact, consult with the angels in making man, and so "Us" refers to God and the angels. Of course, monotheism is predicated upon the emptiness of such a consultation, as there is nothing that the angels could contribute to God's plan. Since God's knowledge is absolute, no other participant could improve His creation of man. So why did God bring in the angels? The rabbis answer that He wanted to set a powerful example for mankind: If all-knowing, all-powerful God indicated a "need" for others, where such a need is axiomatically impossible, certainly we can express our need for our subordinates, who we only *believe* have nothing to contribute.

We may still wonder why such a risky phrase is placed so prominently in the very first chapter of the Torah. It appears that this too is quite deliberate. Ostensibly, creating man is God's most important single act. In working on the most important project or decision of our

---

[1] See, for example, Rav Saadia Gaon and Ramban.

[2] *Bereshit Rabba* 8:8.

lives, would we want to involve those who we feel would not make a positive contribution? Would we not be more tolerant of others' involvement in issues of lesser magnitude? The unlikelihood of a positive answer to the first question requires God to go to great lengths to show us His unequivocal stand about eliciting the participation of our subordinates in our decision-making.

Thus, we are taught a powerful lesson on the nature of humility as well as the obligation to honor others and to show our need for their possible contribution, no matter how unlikely that contribution will be. This lesson could only be taught so dramatically by God's "consulting" with the angels in the creation of man. Yet as the rabbis point out, this lesson comes at a theological cost to us, i.e., that it allows room for polytheists to find support in the Torah for their beliefs.

Most significant is the fact that the cost and benefit described above are inseparable: there was no way to have one without the other. The rabbis are thus indicating that God chose which value was more important. God's choice is not to be understood to mean that the cost was non-existent or even unimportant. Certainly, for someone to entertain doubts about monotheism is far from a trivial matter. Thus, God chose to allow for the negative consequences created rather than to avoid them and in so doing, weaken the teaching of humility that comes from His inclusion of angels in the making of man.

Choosing Sarah's Death

Another example of Divine trade-offs appears in the story of the *Akeida* (Binding of Yitzchak). Avraham is asked to do much more than kill his child. A close reading of the text reveals that God made this trial as difficult as possible. It is based on such a reading that the Midrash embellishes the story, telling us that the *Satan* provided several additional impediments to Avraham's task. But the most difficult part of this trial is that Avraham is asked to destroy his entire identity by eagerly fulfilling the opposite of everything he believes to be good and right.

Apparently, such an extreme test was needed for the development of mankind and of God's chosen nation. Avraham had to show *complete* submission to God in order to be designated as the father of the Jewish people. This, since the Jews would need to show tremendous levels of dedication to succeed in their historical mission. Such dedication could only come through the legacy of someone who had passed the most difficult test of faith ever recorded. Moreover, it is this test which was intended to separate the Jews from all other nations and allow the Jews to make their claim to chosenness. According to rabbinic tradition, it is this test that forces other nations to recognize the superiority of the Jews' commitment because they are the spiritual descendants of the one who was willing to give up everything for the sake of God.[3]

As with the problematic use of the phrase, "Let Us make man," the *Akeida* could not be accomplished without an important trade-off. In *Bereshit* 23:2, the rabbis tell us that when Sarah heard of the *Akeida*, her soul flew out of her body.[4] However we are to understand this, hers is not the portrait of a desirable and timely death. Hearing about Avraham's intention to kill Yitzchak could well have overtaxed Sarah's emotional resources and logically led to her demise. The rabbis are telling us that Sarah could have been an inevitable victim of the events that had just transpired.

If we are to understand the Midrash as recording an actual historical event, it would seem reasonable to say that here, too, God made a necessary trade-off. The test of the *Akeida* could not be

---

[3] See *Tanchuma Yeshana*, Parashat Vayera, 46. It is perhaps for this very reason that Moslem scholars have felt compelled to write that the child bound was actually Yishmael and not Yitzchak, thereby taking away the legacy of the *Akeida* from Judaism and giving it to Islam.

[4] This is based on the juxtaposition of the story of the *Akeida* and the account of Sarah's death and burial (*semichat parashiot*).

accomplished without Sarah dying in the way that she did. In addition to being an inevitable consequence, her death could be one more component of the test itself. As mentioned earlier, God made every facet of Avraham's test as difficult as is possible. Since, according to the Midrash, Sarah's death was an obvious consequence of the *Akeida*, Avraham may well have realized that his killing Yitzchak would likely result in the death of Sarah as well. This thought would have served as one more devastating psychological barrier for Avraham in his test of submission.[5]

In reviewing the example of "Let Us make man," we see that God had to make a choice in the same way that one must choose between black and white, since what is black cannot simultaneously be white. In our example of the *Akeida*, however, it appears that God could have avoided making a choice. Could God not have created miracles to avoid the natural consequences of this event? In other words, couldn't Yitzchak have been put into a trance? Couldn't Sarah have been cut off from all information about what had happened? Surely, this is no more difficult than splitting the Red Sea or creating the world. The apparent

---

[5] Viewing the tangential events surrounding the *Akeida* as additional facets of Avraham's test also solves another problem that has troubled commentators from the Talmudic period to the present: After we read of Avraham and Yitzchak's every action on the way to the *Akeida*, Yitzchak mysteriously disappears (most conspicuously in *Bereshit* 22:19), only to reappear several chapters later. When he reappears, Avraham inexplicably disappears. The next time that they clearly reappear together is at Avraham's funeral. (In *Bereshit* 25:5 when we are told that Avraham gave his inheritance to Yitzchak, that does not imply that he did so in Yitzchak's presence.) Many explanations are tendered, but they all seem forced, or divorced, from the story line. Could it be that Yitzchak did go back home – but without Avraham? After the *Akeida*, the human bond between father and son was forever ruptured. Even though Yitzchak agreed with every action taken by his father, a human being cannot see his father in the act of killing him and remain the same. Yitzchak's associations with his father could no longer be what they were before this pivotal event in both of their lives. Yitzchak's "disappearance" is another indication of the inevitable cost of a test such as the *Akeida*.

reason that God refrained from intervening in the *Akeida* is that it was the only way to allow for the emergence of the lessons meant for the reader. If we are to learn from the actions of the *Avot*, they have to play by the same natural rules that govern our own lives. Otherwise, the reader would be hard-pressed to emulate the resolve of Avraham, given that, as opposed to the common mortal, the Biblical heroes could always expect to be bailed out via supernatural intervention.[6]

Iyov and David

A similar question can be asked about Iyov (Job). In the end of the book of Iyov, the book's namesake is compensated for the death of his original family by being blessed with a new family. One might ask why God would not revive the dead in this particular situation, especially as the death of Iyov's family was primarily intended to test Iyov and not to punish his family. Here too, however, undoing natural (albeit Divinely ordained) events would cheapen Iyov's test and ultimately make it irrelevant for the future, where God would not revive the dead every time someone passes a test of faith.

By not intervening with miracles, God teaches us one of life's most important realities in appropriately dramatic fashion: Great things often come at great cost. This means that making sacrifices is a necessary and expected part of striving for the good and the right. To believe otherwise is a delusion that prevents us from confronting our decisions with open eyes.

Another great Biblical hero forced to deal with the difficult consequences of his proper choices is David. In *Divrei haYamim I* 22:8, David is disqualified from building the Temple as a result of having "blood on his hands." While some commentators understand this blood

---

[6] See Chapter 1, p. 30.

to be of the innocent victims of war,[7] Rashi understands the blood to be a result of fighting essential wars for the benefit of the Jewish people. He continues to explain that any killing, no matter how necessary, is incongruous with the building of the Temple. In other words, David did the right thing in fighting the wars that he did. Nevertheless, doing the right thing came at the great personal cost of disqualification from building the Temple.

As with Avraham, David's correct choices came with an implicit price. There was no other way to achieve the physical security of the Jewish people. Also, as with Avraham, the fact that doing the right thing came at a high personal cost made it all the more heroic. Real heroes are people who make difficult choices and suffer the consequences, not mindless characters who somehow avoid ever making trade-offs – which are an intrinsic part of life as we know it.

Trade-offs in Torah and Halacha

Not only is the concept of trade-offs relevant in deciding between two mutually exclusive options, it may also give us better insight into the nature of virtue and sin as well. If the trade-offs mentioned in the Biblical selections above show how correct choices come with inseparable negative consequences, could we not likely find examples of the converse? In other words, could it not be that negative choices come with inseparable positive consequences?[8] If so, it would follow that some acts proscribed by the Torah may actually also contain some good.

The concept that sin often has a positive component may well be the central issue associated with the Tree of Knowledge of Good and Evil. It seems that what ultimately convinced Chava to eat from the tree

---

[7] See, for example, Redak.

[8] See, for example, Rabbi J.B. Soloveitchik's explanation of the positive dynamic ultimately put into motion by sin in his discussion of *teshuva* in Pinchas Peli, *Al haTeshuva* (Jerusalem: World Zionist Organization, 1985) pp. 175–87.

was its apparent beauty and practical utility as food.[9] This surprised Chava – her expectation must have been that something forbidden by God would have no redeeming qualities.[10] Unfortunately for Chava, however, such an understanding of good and evil is incorrect; or rather, it is only correct as an understanding of pristine, absolute good and evil. It is not an accurate understanding of how evil presents itself in this world.[11]

This means that we can, and should, ascribe value to those acts we choose to forgo, and, on some level, even mourn their inevitable loss. When we keep Shabbat by not listening to recorded music, it is not to say that listening to such music is devoid of spiritual value. Rather, it is a value that is outweighed by the spiritual benefits of keeping to the discipline of Shabbat prohibitions and the sanctity thereby created. Likewise, when we break Shabbat in order to save a life, it comes at the high price of transgressing the sanctity of Shabbat. We do so because the value of human life is greater than the very special value of Shabbat observance, and not because that sanctity somehow mysteriously disappears while we are in the process of saving a life.

In fact, the corpus of halacha deals extensively with mutually exclusive, competing values (i.e., if I am studying Torah and other mitzvot come up, which one do I give up for the sake of the other?). This indicates that most halachic decisions can be viewed as the examination of the moral and spiritual trade-offs created by our choices. Viewed from this perspective, Torah law can be viewed as a religious cost/benefit analysis.

Halacha can be seen as a guide to decision-making in general. Many halachic choices we face, such as the ones suggested above, are a

---

[9] *Bereshit* 3:6.

[10] See Ramban, *Bereshit* 3:6. This unexpected cognitive dissonance seems to be what made an ostensibly simple test a very sophisticated one indeed.

[11] This is also how Seforno (*Bereshit* 3:7) apparently understands the transformation that occurred in Adam's and Chava's perceptions as a result of eating from the tree.

question of choosing the better good, not defining one value as good and the other one as bad. On one level this makes it more difficult for us to make choices; when we realize that choices are not absolute, it requires greater responsibility. On another level, however, understanding the trade-offs implicit in most choices frees us from the terrible burden of negating value in what we choose not to do, even though we intuitively know that such value exists. Such an understanding inherently creates a much higher level of appropriate intellectual tolerance for those who make choices different from our own. Moreover, it appears that such tolerance is precisely what is indicated by a close reading of the Bible.

Moral Complexity

As children, we may have thought that the choices made by our Biblical patriarchs and matriarchs were simple ones. A more mature and careful analysis will reveal that this is rarely the case, and that these choices are often more complex than we realize: Whereas in the previous section, it became clear that choices are inevitable, we will now see that choices often involve a large number of components, making them both complicated and nuanced.

Holy Marital Strife

One often unexamined aspect of Lavan's switching Leah for Rachel[12] is the role of Leah herself in her father's plot. Some commentators, however, do raise the issue of whether Leah was justified in going along with it.[13] Rabbi Samson Raphael Hirsch suggests that she had no choice, yet if this were truly the case it is hard to imagine that Leah would not

---

[12] *Bereshit* 29:22–26.

[13] See Ramban, *Bereshit* 29:30, Rabbi S.R. Hirsch, ibid., Da'at Zekenim, *Bereshit* 29:25.

have revealed her identity once she was alone with Yaakov – unless she was a willing party to the deception. Rabbinic tradition suggests just such a scenario, telling us that Leah acquired a secret code known only to Yaakov and Rachel specifically in order to conceal her identity until after the marriage was consummated.[14] According to this tradition, then, not only did Leah not resist being a party to her father's scheme, she was an active accomplice to it.

A surprising midrash speaks to this point. According to this midrash, the following is the conversation that ensued from Yaakov's discovery that the woman he had just married was not Rachel but Leah: Yaakov said to Leah, "You are a liar, the daughter of a liar – last night, I called you Rachel and you answered me; now I call you Leah and you also answer me!" She said back to him, "Are you a man with no students? Your father called you Esav and you answered him, and then he called you Yaakov and you also answered him!"[15]

The midrash reveals a truly fascinating comparison of Leah's deception of Yaakov with Yaakov's own deception of his father, Yitzchak. In both cases, there are at least six points of comparison: 1) one sibling pretends to be the other; 2) the deception is instigated by a parent; 3) the deception ends up to be for the good of everyone involved, in spite of the emotional anguish it causes its victim; 4) there was no time to wait – not acting would have been as much a choice as acting; 5) the victim (Yitzchak and Yaakov) was fooled because he could not see, one

---

[14] *Megila* 13b. Granted, the sages are more interested in Rachel's behavior in this passage, wherein Leah's motivation seems to come from wanting to avoid personal embarrassment, but the clear implication remains that Leah wants to avoid detection by Yaakov.

[15] *Agadot Bereshit*, Chap. 48, quoted by Da'at Zekenim, *op. cit.* See also *Bereshit Rabba* 70:19.

on account of his blindness, the other because of the dark of night;[16] 6) the deception appeared to be the only way of accomplishing an important goal – Ramban argues that Yitzchak was intent on giving the blessing to Esav and that no one could have dissuaded him. As a result, Rivka sought to direct the blessing to Yaakov with the only method at her disposal.[17] Similarly, Yaakov was only interested in marrying Rachel, who, if we follow the story carefully, was less suited than Leah to be his wife.[18] Following in her mother-in-law's footsteps, Leah used the only method at her disposal to get Yaakov to enter into this critical marriage.

Returning to the midrash, it would be difficult to say that Leah was simply chiding Yaakov by telling him that he got what he deserved. More likely, Leah was telling Yaakov that the morality of the two situations was very similar. Since he presumably thought that he was justified in doing what he did, and that the importance of truth was outweighed by other considerations, he should see her dishonesty in a similar light.

Such a claim would be reinforced by normative halacha, which does not view truth as indispensable in all circumstances. Some superseding values such as domestic harmony take precedence over the prohibition of lying. The rabbis actually prove this by claiming that God Himself changed Sarah's words so as not to get Avraham upset with her. Sarah expressed amazement that God could give them a child despite

---

[16] I am indebted to my student, Dana Pulver, for this keen observation. The observation also seems to be made by Leon Kass in *The Beginnings of Wisdom* (Chicago: University of Chicago Press, 2003) pp. 423–24.

[17] Ramban, *Bereshit* 27:4.

[18] After all, the vast majority of the Jewish people, as well as its religious and political leadership, all come from Leah and not from Rachel. See Rabbenu Bachya, *Bereshit* 28:1, who suggests that Yaakov may have even been punished for his incorrect desire to marry Rachel and not Leah.

Avraham's advanced age. In reporting this to Avraham, God says that Sarah expressed wonder because of her own old age.[19]

Thus, both situations discussed above involved difficult moral decisions, wherein the right choice was not clear. There was no good choice, or at least no perfect one. For Yaakov not to act would have meant allowing Esav to acquire much more power with which to afflict Yaakov and his descendants. It would also have meant forgoing the significant spiritual advantages of his father's blessing. Acting involved deceiving Yitzchak, violating his dictates and causing him tremendous grief.

Likewise, had Leah not deceived Yaakov, he would never have married her, and the majority of the Jewish people never would have seen the light of day. Acting involved Leah's deceiving her new husband, thereby starting her marriage on a note of discord. Indeed, the family life of Yaakov would by mired by jealousy and rivalry for almost the entirety of his life.

What is true of Leah and Yaakov is really true of all our Biblical heroes. The predicaments they faced did not come with facile solutions. When Avraham and Yitzchak vulnerably came to foreign nations accompanied by unusually beautiful wives,[20] there were no easy solutions. When Yosef had to deal with the jealousy of his holy brothers, there were also no easy solutions. The more we think about it, the more we will see that most of the choices faced by our ancestors were quite complex.

The Wisdom of Maximizing Opportunities

By highlighting the difficulty of these two decisions – i.e., Yaakov's decision to listen to his mother and Leah's decision to listen to her father – the above-mentioned midrash teaches us two important points:

---

[19] *Yevamot* 65b, commenting on *Bereshit* 18:13.

[20] *Bereshit* 12:10–15, 20:1–2 and 26:6–7.

Most decisions do not involve clear choices, and not acting is as much of a decision as acting.[21]

There are many practical situations where we foolishly wait for simpler choices. One popular example is singles who have a shopping list of what they are looking for in a spouse. If the person they meet doesn't have everything on the list, they would rather wait. What they sometimes learn is that waiting only forces them to face more complex choices, wherein a different part of the list is missing. The result is missed opportunities to take advantage of the real choices offered all of us by life.

Another familiar example exists in our financial dealings. Traders will often want to buy or sell a stock at a certain price, and only at that price. Since this does not always correspond to the available choices, it can be counterproductive. By waiting for the stock to go down to a certain price, we often lose the opportunity to buy a stock that, although not as cheap as we would want, is still a good deal. As the Torah teaches us through our patriarchs and matriarchs, it is important to understand that "perfect" choices rarely present themselves.

In French, there's an expression: *Le mieux est l'enemi du bien,* which means, "The enemy of good is better." In other words, waiting for the ideal is the best way to lose out on most opportunities that come our way. This is different from saying that we should settle for mediocrity. Of course we should always seek the best in everything we do, but since

---

21 Granted, the rabbis recommend the principle of *shev ve'al ta'aseh adif* – when in doubt, it is better to refrain from action. They do not, however, tell us to follow this principle until we are completely sure that it is better to act. Rather, they are describing a situation about which, in spite of our best efforts to resolve the doubt, we remain basically in the dark as to what is the proper course of action. In such a case, all other things being equal, the rabbis tell us that we have less to lose by mistaken inaction than by mistaken action.

most things are not in our control, we have to be ready to deal with the realities that confront us *as they are*, and not as we would like them to be.

God has given us the wisdom to deal with complex choices. This is true in our social lives, our business lives and our religious lives. If we have time for only one Torah class a week, we shouldn't say, "Why bother? I'll wait until I retire, when I can really devote serious time to Torah study." We should take advantage of the opportunities available to us right now.

We spend far too much of our lives waiting for perfection. Like Yaakov and Leah, we have to seize opportunities, even if they are not ideal. If we think back on our own difficult choices, we will see that making them is often what has allowed us to grow as human beings.

Torah and Fantasy

A ninth-grade student once complained to me that our Torah is not so interesting compared to the various mythologies of ancient peoples. On the level of adventure and fantasy, there may be some truth to this. I told him there is a reason for that – the Torah is about real life, whereas mythology is all in someone's imagination. In the world of mythology and fairly tales, we can turn into a prince, marry a fairy princess and live happily ever after. Our Torah, however, is not interested in entertaining our imagination. Instead, it is interested in steering us to better and more meaningful lives. As such, its stories are filled with situations meant to be instructive.

In the first section of this chapter, we saw several narratives showing the inevitability of choice. Like it or not, by striving to attain certain goals, we are automatically giving up on others. On a simple level, this is the nature of finite time and space. But it goes deeper than that: becoming one type of person precludes us from becoming a different type of person because there are also limitations and choices concerning the human psyche.

We define ourselves by our actions and thoughts. As we define ourselves, our memories and habits automatically mold us into who we are – and prevent us from becoming something completely at odds with our emotional and intellectual choices. Yet it is true that we can use the experiences that create our personalities in different ways. A well-known example of this is the person who repents out of love for God (*ba'al teshuva me'ahava*). He is apparently able to use the sins of his past as a way to come closer to his Creator.[22] Nonetheless, one thing we cannot do is to completely *erase* our memories and habits.

In the second section, we discussed the complexity of choice and the responsibility that comes with it. Looking beneath the story line, we see that our heroes in the Tanakh had to deal with complex decisions. In fact, making complex decisions is exactly that which transforms a person into a hero. Anyone can make an obvious choice between clear good and evil. It takes a person of heightened spiritual stature and wisdom, however, to make successful choices when good and evil are nuanced. Perhaps this is what our sages meant when they said that there is no rest for the very righteous (*tzaddikim*).[23] A *tzaddik* is precisely the one who is engaged in making difficult decisions. He is the one constantly addressing the problems and choices of his time with an appreciation of the complexity attached to every situation that comes before him.

In our own fantasy world, we want moral choices to be pristine; we expect to do mitzvot in the ideal situation, where we have all the time, money and inspiration in the world. It is for this reason that we have to learn from the *Avot* and *Imahot* that we live in the real world, where choices are not comfortable and easy. When we accept this truth, we can greet the choices facing us in modern society with appreciation. As with

---

[22] *Yoma* 86b.

[23] *Berachot* 64a.

our Biblical heroes, confronting the complexity of decisions is what allows us to grow. Although the many choices we face in the context of modern life may mitigate the leisure we think we want, they can be an important catalyst toward becoming the people we should be.

CHAPTER 3

Redeeming Our Nation:
Yishmael and Yisrael

One idea propounded by the *mussar* movement is the elusiveness as well as the centrality of self-knowledge. Because our lack of objectivity with regard to ourselves is a major obstacle to self-knowledge, it is often easier to learn about ourselves by observing the character and behavior of others. We are less likely to be swayed by subjectivity in this case. Likewise, we can learn much about the Jewish nation by comparing Yaakov (Yisrael), the Jewish Biblical prototype, to other major personalities in the Bible. One particularly powerful example of such a contrast is that between Yisrael and Yishmael, the classical prototype of Moslem Arab civilization.

In this chapter, we will focus on how the Torah understands the Jewish nation in contrast to Yishmael. This will allow us to better understand what is expected of us and see how well we measure up to this standard. At the same time, we will perforce also come to a better understanding of Yishmael, obtaining insight and direction in dealing with his "descendants."

With regard to Yishmael's "descendants," it is appropriate to start with a very important caveat often ignored. R. Avraham ibn Ezra convincingly argues that the Arabs are not genealogically descended from Yishmael, nor is Christian Europe descended from Esav.[1] Inasmuch as

---

[1] Ibn Ezra on *Bereshit* 27:40.

the rabbis were aware of this, their midrashic association of Yishmael with the Arabs is presumably only rooted in the characteristics of Yishmael, and not in the actual physical person. In other words, the rabbis noticed basic character traits in Yishmael that reminded them of national traits evident in the Arab nation. Likewise with Esav and Christian Europe. Thus, any qualities the rabbis ascribe to "Yishmael" are attributes passed down through culture. They were not speaking about genetic predetermination of physical descendants.

Another important caveat must be stated. As already mentioned in the Introduction, since we want the *text* to speak to us, we have to put our biases aside and attempt an objective analysis of the text. This is especially significant in dealing with Yishmael as the prototype of the Arab nation, since many of us carry heavy emotional baggage due to the current Arab-Israeli conflict. Yet it is precisely because the matter is of so much concern that we are in greatest need of the Torah's help in how to understand the issues. Thus, in order to get truly text-based perspectives, we must redouble our efforts to analyze the text objectively.

The Road to Avraham, The Road from Avraham

Most of the narrative about Yishmael is connected to his mother Hagar. In the story of Yishmael's expulsion from the house of Avraham, he is immediately and for no obvious reason referred to as the son of Hagar. Almost inexplicably, Hagar is then meted out the same fate of expulsion as her son.[2] In this narrative, which is ostensibly about Yishmael, Hagar somehow proceeds to take center stage. This leads us to the conclusion that the Torah clearly wants us to notice the tight intertwining of the characters and fates of these two seminal personalities. As we shall see, a

---

[2] *Bereshit* 21:9–10. This issue is raised by many commentators. Also of interest is that Sarah speaks about expelling Hagar even before she mentions expelling Yishmael.

close reading of the text will reveal many common threads between them. The text introduces us to Hagar with the following narrative.

> Sarai the wife of Avram took Hagar the Egyptian, her maidservant, at the end of ten years of Avram's dwelling in the land of Canaan, and she gave her to Avram her husband as a wife. He came to Hagar and she became pregnant. She saw that she had become pregnant and her mistress became light in her eyes. Sarai said to Avram, "My injury is upon you – I gave you my maidservant into your lap, she saw that she became pregnant and I became light in her eyes; God should judge between us...." Avram said to Sarai, "Here is your maidservant in your hand – do to her what is good in your eyes." Sarai afflicted her and she ran away from her.
>
> An angel of God found her... he said, "Hagar, maidservant of Sarai, from where have you come and to where are you going?" She said, "I am running away from Sarai, my mistress." An angel of God said to her, "Go back to your mistress and allow yourself to be afflicted by her hand." An angel of God said to her, "I will greatly increase your seed, it will not be countable on account of its great size." An angel of God said to her, "Behold, you are pregnant and you will give birth to a son and you will call his name Yishmael, since God heard your affliction. He will be a wild man, his hand will be in all and the hand of all will be in him and he will dwell [near] all his brothers." She called the name of God Who was speaking to her, You are the God Who sees me. (*Bereshit* 16:3–13)

In Hagar we see great paradoxes. Seemingly a woman of tremendous stature, there are also fatal flaws in her character. On some level, her elevated status can be ascertained by her very union with Avraham: the care taken in choosing the future spouses of Yitzchak and

Yaakov shows that finding an appropriate mother for the early Jewish progeny was not taken lightly. The rabbis, however, cite further evidence of her status. After she runs away from Sarah's harsh treatment, she encounters an angel who announces the future birth of Yishmael. The text formulates her interaction with the angel in a manner that alludes to the actual presence of several angels. The multiplicity of angels and her matter-of-fact response give the impression that she was quite comfortable with the presence of lofty spiritual beings.[3] Even as the rabbis point out that this familiarity with angels came as the result of living in the house of Avraham, what they likely mean is that her spiritual growth was immeasurably advanced by her proximity to Avraham and Sarah. Whatever the reason for it, however, the ability to converse with angels is almost always an indication of a high spiritual level.

The rabbis' reading of the text further supports this contention, suggesting that Ketura – whom Avraham married after the death of Sarah – was a new name for Hagar.[4] Moreover, the rabbis suggest that this new name is meant to allude to her elevated behavior.[5] Granted, our sages also suggest that she strayed and worshiped idols once she left Avraham's house.[6] Nonetheless, in the cultural context of the times, this should not come as a surprise. (It has been suggested that the same fate met the "converts" of Avraham and Sarah once they left the couple's inspiring presence.) Consequently, whether or not we accept that Ketura was Hagar according to the simple reading of the text,[7] it is clear that Hagar is far from being a Biblical villainess.

---

[3] *Bereshit Rabba* 45:7.

[4] Ibid., 61:5.

[5] The name Ketura is understood to be a derivative of the Hebrew word *ketoret*, sweet-smelling incense.

[6] *Pirkei deRabbi Eliezer* 30.

[7] Rashi accepts this to be the simple meaning of *Bereshit* 25:1, while Rashbam and Ibn Ezra do not.

In spite of this, Hagar's behavior is also problematic at certain points in the narrative. Even though several commentators blame Sarah for her treatment of Hagar,[8] Hagar does not come off blameless. The text itself indicates the questionable nature of her losing esteem for her "mistress" (i.e., her superior). The rabbis, however, assume her train of thought to be completely logical: Hagar did not believe that a physiological barrier was keeping Sarah from giving birth. Given that God was directly involved in the process, Hagar came to the conclusion that there was something beneath the surface that was wrong with Sarah. After all, on the face of it, Sarah seemed to be a very righteous woman. It must be that God saw something negative in Sarah, about which no one else knew. By comparison, Hagar's conceiving seemed to prove that she had found favor in God's eyes.[9] This understandable conclusion made Hagar look down upon Sarah.

Hagar's train of thought as formulated by the rabbis is not meant to whitewash her. For one, it shows her to be self-righteous. As we shall see, the tendency among Jewish Biblical heroes is to underestimate their own righteousness, not inflate it.[10] In contrast to this, Hagar displays a certain amount of arrogance foreign to the Jewish spirit. The rabbinical contention that she was born of royal lineage[11] may help to explain this flaw, but does not exonerate it.

Like Mother, Like Son

This character flaw of Hagar's is also manifest in her son. Just as Hagar is too easily convinced of her superiority to Sarah, Yishmael, too,

---

[8] Most notably, Ramban on *Bereshit* 16:6.

[9] *Bereshit Rabba* 45:5.

[10] See Chapter 6, p. 112 ff.

[11] *Bereshit Rabba* 45:1.

apparently draws the conclusion that he is greater than his younger brother, Yitzchak. In fact, we shall see indications that his greatest challenge may well have been suppressing his superiority complex.

The Talmud states that Yishmael repented and became a righteous man,[12] and the proof text for this is quite telling. The rabbis point to the fact that Avraham was buried by "Yitzchak and Yishmael."[13] This is compared to Yitzchak's burial, which was performed by "Esav and Yaakov."[14] In the first case, the text lists the younger brother first, whereas in the second the older brother comes first. The rabbis extrapolate from the order of the names that by the time Avraham was buried, Yishmael recognized his own inferiority to Yitzchak. On the face of it, that does not make someone into a righteous man. One could be a murderer, a thief or all sorts of other things and still recognize the superiority of a Yitzchak. Apparently, however, this act of subordination is what determined Yishmael's righteousness.

As with Hagar, perhaps we can assume that Yishmael, being part of Avraham's household, was basically righteous.[15] Yet, like Hagar, he has difficulty in realistically evaluating himself. This can be seen in the Biblical text. Yishmael is sent out of his home for either laughing or scorning. Many commentators[16] view Avraham's preference for Yitzchak as the likely subject of Yishmael's attitude and behavior. In this context, scorn represents Yishmael's derision for Avraham's "lack of wisdom" in favoring Yitzchak.

Yishmael is then thrown out of his home, which confirms Avraham's preference for Yitzchak over Yishmael. No doubt, it is always difficult for an older brother to cede any advantage to a younger brother.

---

[12] *Baba Batra* 16b.

[13] *Bereshit* 25:9.

[14] Ibid., 35:29.

[15] See *Tosefta, Sota* 6:3, where R. Shimon bar Yochai makes this very point.

[16] Such as Ramban and Seforno.

Moreover, in this case, Yishmael is losing all standing in the family whatsoever. More than anything else, then, the rabbis saw this as Yishmael's challenge. If Yitzchak had to accept that Avraham knew what he was doing when he was going to slaughter him, Yishmael had to accept that Avraham knew what he was doing when he placed Yitzchak in the position normally conferred upon the firstborn son. Thus, when Yishmael acquiesces to Yitzchak's leadership in the burial of their father, he is understood to have redressed the critical scorn he had shown for his father's preference of Yitzchak.

Limited Submission[17]

A thorough examination of the text reveals other flaws in Hagar's character besides the feelings of superiority mentioned earlier. Such an examination of *Bereshit* 16:7–14 reveals Hagar's problematic reticence to listen to the angel(s) sent to direct her back to Avraham's home. Whether it indicates a multiplicity of angels or not, the Torah's repeating "And the angel said to her" does indicate some sort of pause after each phrase, as if we are expecting Hagar to react.[18] In other words, each statement should be enough to get Hagar to return back home, but she resists until the final promise, that her son's character will somehow compensate for her

---

[17] The Arabic word, *Islam*, means submission. Hagar and Yishmael actually are able to submit to many difficult demands placed upon them. The purpose of this section is to point out their weaknesses, without losing sight of their strengths. Thus, I would like to compare their response to the demands of heaven with the response of those viewed as the founders of the Jewish people, such as Avraham and Yitzchak. Lest some readers understand this section as a gratuitous attack on Islam, I would encourage them to place this section within the context of the entire chapter.

[18] Many commentators point this out. See, for example, Abarbanel and Malbim.

situation. This is in marked contrast to Avraham's immediate acquiescence to the Divine demands placed upon him to sacrifice his son.

We see Hagar's reluctance to show complete self-sacrifice later when she and Yishmael are thrown out of Avraham's home. When it appears that Yishmael is about to die, Hagar does something very strange. In *Bereshit* 21:16 she moves away from her child, stating that she does not want to see him die. Granted, such a sight is horrific, but what about Yishmael? Would he not expect his mother to stand by him in his final moments? Apparently, when such difficult demands are made of her, Hagar chooses to follow the path of personal comfort.[19]

It is not clear from the text whether Yishmael follows his mother in her reluctance to emulate Avraham's complete submission. Rabbinic tradition, however, seems to lean in this very direction. In a fascinating midrashic discussion between Yitzchak and Yishmael, the latter boasts about having undergone circumcision when he was old enough to resist, as opposed to Yitzchak who underwent it as a baby. Yitzchak responds by saying, if God were to ask me now to submit myself to slaughter, I would willingly acquiesce.[20] As in all such debates, the winner is the one who can make the greatest claim. Yishmael's silence at this point in the discussion allows Yitzchak to show his greater will to submission. Thus, what the rabbis are indicating is that Yishmael, like his mother, was not willing to take religious devotion to its logical extreme of complete submission. He was willing to sacrifice much, but not everything, for the sake of heaven. A similar contention is made about his spiritual descendants, who first want to know what is in the Torah before deciding whether or not to accept it.[21]

---

[19] See Rabbi S.R. Hirsch on *Bereshit* 21:15–16.

[20] *Sanhedrin* 79b.

[21] *Sifrei* on *Devarim* 33:2, *Avoda Zara* 2b.

Yishmael the Victim

A third behavioral theme common to both Hagar and Yishmael is the temptation to view themselves as victims. As mentioned earlier, some classical Jewish commentators understand the text as telling us that Hagar really was victimized by Sarah. Indeed, the word the Torah uses for Sarah's treatment of Hagar is the same word used for the treatment of the Jewish slaves in Egypt. Even if we accept such a view, however, it apparently does not condone Hagar's thinking of herself as a victim entitled to compensation. The angel that represents the Divine will points out that she remains Sarah's maidservant and that she must go back to meet her fate. He is not denying that she was mistreated, but neither does he directly relate to her suffering. Rather, by not relating to it and sending her back, he may be telling her to pursue a different path in dealing with her oppression. Whereas Hagar was quick to view Sarah with derision as a result of her childlessness, Hagar was less ready to see if she had any responsibility for her own fate. As explained most clearly by Rambam, the Jewish response to calamity is introspection.[22] A Jew must ask himself, "What might *I* have done to bring this upon myself?" We are certainly allowed to defend ourselves against others, but dwelling on their misdeeds is counterproductive. It is far more productive to analyze our own mistakes and try to understand what we can do to improve. Thus, while protecting ourselves against others is a way to preserve our bodies, introspection is a way to preserve our souls, which is of much greater consequence.

Yishmael is also put in a situation where he can choose to feel victimized. If Avraham's preference for Yitzchak were not bad enough, the manner in which Yishmael is sent out of his home could easily have created a desire for Yishmael to permanently estrange himself from his family. From this perspective, Yishmael's greatest challenge goes beyond acknowledging his position of relative inferiority. His greatest challenge

---

[22] *Mishneh Torah*, Hilchot Ta'anit 1:1–3.

becomes suppressing the natural inclination to forever seek redress for the injustice he certainly must have felt. Yet only after suppressing this inclination could he objectively compare his own merits to those of Yitzchak. The spiritual greatness of Yishmael lay in his success in doing just this. Not only does Yishmael outwardly meet the challenge of allowing his younger brother to take the lead in burying his father, he also displays his inner peace with the situation by allowing his own daughter Machalat to marry Avraham's grandson, Esav,[23] thereby forever reinforcing his own connection to Yitzchak's family.

While the main point of this chapter is Jewish self-definition, one cannot help but think that Yishmael's challenge may also be the major challenge of the Arab world today. After all, there are certainly different possible perspectives on how to understand their conflict with the Jewish nation. Like Yishmael, the Arabs could legitimately claim to be the victims, the ones who were first, only to be subsequently mistreated by the world and sent away. In the Torah we see that Yishmael only prevails when he pushes such a claim aside and subordinates himself to Yitzchak. One wonders if it is not just such an attitudinal change that is needed to bring about an end to the political conflict in the Middle East.

It would not be surprising if the ability of the Arabs to pursue their calling as partners in the march toward ethical monotheism[24] will be determined by their ability to overcome the victim syndrome. That the Arab masses are more religious than other peoples may well be the case, but so long as they play the victim and focus on the misdeeds of others instead of their own, they will be forever doomed to a moral mediocrity, unbecoming of the "descendants" of Avraham.

---

[23] *Bereshit* 28:9.

[24] Regarding this role of Islam from a Jewish perspective, see *Mishnah Torah*, Hilchot Melachim 1:4 (uncensored version).

Yishmael the *Ba'al Teshuva*

Whether it was great or small, it appears that it was Yishmael's misbehavior that caused Avraham to send him away. As such, when the text later hints to Yishmael's righteousness, the rabbis say that he repented. Like his mother, Yishmael is not a uniformly righteous individual. In this way he differs from his half-brother Yitzchak. It is precisely because of this difference, however, that Yishmael gives us an alternative approach to religiosity which is well worth our attention.

Hagar, at least according to the rabbis, is a woman who moves back and forth on her spiritual road. Her tenure in the house of Avraham is interrupted by two declines. The first of these occurs when she becomes pregnant, prompting her to demean Sarah. The second happens when she is thrown out of Avraham's home together with Yishmael, which, as mentioned, is seen as a return to the polytheism of her youth. Each time, however, she returns to the home and to the ways of Avraham, which, when put all together, gives the impression that Hagar went through a protracted spiritual struggle. This, as opposed to David, who is usually presented as the classical *ba'al teshuva* (penitent). In his case, he falls when he takes Bat Sheva from her first husband, Uriah, and this occurs only once and is quickly recognized. By comparison, Hagar appears to experience constant moral struggle throughout her life.

Hagar's Egyptian background makes such a struggle completely expected. In the Torah, there is a clear association between Egypt and immorality. Most telling is Avraham's expectation that it would be well nigh impossible to protect Sarah's chastity when living in Egypt,[25] which apparently would not have been the case in most other places. The Torah emphasizes Hagar's origins, introducing her as an Egyptian and then repeating this fact a few verses later. The text subsequently reminds us of her nationality when telling us that Yishmael, her son, was engaging in problematic laughter or scorn. In the latter case, Egypt seems to be

---

[25] *Bereshit* 12:11–15.

mentioned as a partial explanation for, or cultural context to, Yishmael's behavior. Here, Egypt is mentioned in contradistinction to the morality that Avraham was trying to bring into the world. As such, Hagar may well have had the occasional longings of many contemporary *ba'alei teshuva* for the pleasures of immorality that they once knew from close up. Given Hagar's Egyptian background, the rabbis' reading of the text that portrays Hagar as a conflicted individual is a very likely reading indeed.

As opposed to his mother, Yishmael only sins once and thus only repents once. His sin and consequent repentance concerns his attitude toward Yitzchak. Nevertheless, his is not the immediate repentance of a David who right away seeks to redress his wrongs or even that of a Shaul who, although he first denies his wrong, is also not slow to repent. The text does not inform us when Yishmael changed his attitude, the result of which we only see much later. Yet Yishmael's absence from the text until Avraham's burial gives the impression that such a development was not an overnight affair.[26] It is likely that this fact is the springboard for the midrashim that speak about a long drawn-out process overseen by Avraham from afar.[27]

Yisrael or Yishmael – Who Are We?

The moral and spiritual struggle experienced by Hagar and Yishmael may have its roots in their lack of complete submission. Struggle is largely a result of indecision in the prioritization of values. Since, as we saw earlier, Hagar and Yishmael may not have been prepared to completely submit to

---

[26] The well-known midrash in *Bereshit Rabba* 33:14 declares that Yishmael was righteous even when he was expelled, but it is likely from the context of this midrash that the term "righteous" here is not telling us that he had achieved spiritual greatness, but rather that, in spite of his flaws, he was basically righteous and thus should not be left to die as the angels wanted.

[27] *Pirkei deRabbi Eliezer* 30.

God's will, they underwent a protracted decision-making process that caused them constant tension. Within the context of this struggle, however, Yishmael shows us the elevated status of one who is not willing to cede the fight to his baser instincts.

As we shall see in Chapter 4, Esav also finds himself in a similar predicament for the same reason – he too is conflicted about how to relate to his brother Yaakov. Yishmael, however, is successful where Esav is not. We shall see that the important positive potential in Esav remains largely latent, in spite of the fact that Esav is of purer lineage than Yishmael. Perhaps one could explain the difference in outcomes by exploring how their respective shortcomings were addressed by their respective fathers. From this perspective, sending Yishmael out of the home may have been the best thing that Avraham ever did for him. In contrast, Esav's behavior was indulged, and therefore he never got the jolt needed to reconsider his actions. Certainly, there are other significant experiential differences to which we can attribute the differences in the outcome of these two personalities. Such a discussion, however, is not directly relevant to our analysis. Of greater interest to us is the fact that Yishmael distinguishes himself in a manner that Esav does not.

Even before Yishmael's birth, his name is chosen by God, a distinction shared with very few others.[28] More striking, however, is that Yishmael is imprinted with Godliness: Who would have expected that Yishmael explicitly bears God's name in the last two letters of his own, something which even his half-brother Yitzchak didn't merit? Beyond his name, Yishmael is also one of the very first to impress the Divine commandment of circumcision onto his own flesh. In this way, he internalizes his allegiance to God, even as he sometimes expresses his reservations. The religious success of Yishmael is rooted, then, in his constant internal pull to do that which God expects of him.

---

[28] See Jerusalem Talmud, *Berachot* 1:6, where the rabbis note that this is a distinction shared with only three other great individuals.

In this context, we should point out that the key to the success of both Yishmael and Yisrael (Yaakov) is the internalization of Godliness, so that the pull to self-transcending morality is strong enough to offset the inborn, natural human drive for selfish physical gain. Yishmael, however, will remain a more universal role model than Yisrael, since the absolute self-sacrifice that Avraham channels through Yitzchak to Yisrael is a quality only expected of the religious vanguard that the Jewish people is meant to be. As such, it may be no coincidence that the people who claim descent from Yishmael have done more to propagate a fierce loyalty to God than anyone else, perhaps including the descendants of Yisrael.[29]

Yisrael also carries the Divine imprint in his name. Consequently, Yishmael and Yisrael share a tremendous common purpose, even as they live apart. The critical difference, however, is Yisrael's tradition of total self-sacrifice, which he inherited from Avraham and Yitzchak. Indeed, according to one rabbinic tradition, the whole point of the binding of Yitzchak was to expose this difference between the true followers of Avraham and all other nations:[30] We do not expect the gentile nations to ask, "Why can't we be tested like Avraham?"[31] The reason this question is not likely to be asked is because total submission is a national legacy unique to the Jews.

Indeed, the sacrifice of one generation after another of Jews for the sake of God is an intrinsic part of Jewish history. It is the nobility of the Jewish nation that makes it willing to give up everything for the sake of God. This is not to say that no other nation has ever been able to do the same, or that all Jews have always attained such a level. Rather, Avraham and Yitzchak passed on the notion of submission as a basic tenet in their approach to God. Armed with a spiritual inheritance that

---

[29] See Rabbi S.R. Hirsch, *Bereshit* 16:14.

[30] *Tanchuma Yashan*, Parashat Vayera 46.

[31] *Tanchuma*, Parashat Balak 1.

includes such an idea, sacrifice may well come more naturally to the Jew. Still, the Jewish people have always allowed anyone who can make a commitment to total self-sacrifice to enter the fold. Once a convert has done so, he is referred to as a *son of Avraham*, our father.

*　　*　　*

It is difficult for many modern Jews to consider the complete self-sacrifice of our ancestors. Therefore, some would view Yishmael as a more likely role model for themselves. Perhaps they would admit to a lack of clarity in their priorities and would thus be happy to attain the internalization of Godliness represented by Yishmael. Even if that would be an important accomplishment on the individual level, we must understand that such a position is a tremendous indictment of the Jews on a national level. If we mentioned that the cultural descendants of Yishmael are not living up to his legacy, we must also admit that not many of the physical descendants of Avraham, Yitzchak and Yisrael are living up to their own legacy. As mentioned earlier, God's special relationship with the Jewish people is predicated precisely upon this legacy of complete submission.[32] Therefore, it is essential for Jews to try to attain our forefathers' clarity of faith, even as we have been completely overwhelmed by a modern cultural climate that is increasingly agnostic.

On the individual level, we may need to first take the path of Yishmael in order to be victorious in our struggle to lead a Godly life. As descendants of Yisrael, however, we may not stop there. Being a Jew requires us to build ourselves into bastions of faith, even as faith has almost never been more out of style. In our struggle against the cultural tides, we also benefit from the legacy of Avraham who manifested an intense faith – specifically in a culture where monotheism had been supplanted by an almost universal paganism. Though our struggle will be

---

[32] See *Avot* 2:5.

almost as difficult as that of Avraham, the Jewish nation's fate is to go beyond the not insignificant legacy of Yishmael to the super-heroic discipline of Yishmael's father. This is the legacy that Avraham bequeathed uniquely to his son Yitzchak and, through him, to Yisrael and his descendants.

A final speculation may be in order. If contemporary Jews can only aspire to the level of Yishmael, can the Jewish nation really expect Divine protection from others who also evoke the legacy of Yishmael? If the Jewish nation has come to expect Divine help in its revival on its ancient soil, certainly it must strive to live up to the legacy that brought about such Divine favor in the first place.

CHAPTER 4

Redeeming Our Genius:
Understanding Yitzchak

Jewish sociologists and historians have written about the highly unusual percentage of Orthodox men studying in *yeshivot*, *kollelim* and other similar institutions in our time. The proliferation of adult Torah study has certainly created greater knowledge and awareness of Talmud and halacha among the Jewish masses. Yet of particular interest is the paradoxical disunity that this trend has created within the Jewish people as to who should be studying and for how long. Of note is the fact that extreme positions on this issue have become quite popular. On the one hand, it is not uncommon to hear the opinion that every Jewish male should ideally study full-time for his entire adult life. On the other hand, others argue that all adult men who are exclusively involved in Torah study are irresponsible parasites.

In this context of very disparate views, it is worthwhile to gently put our prejudices aside and look at the insights on this topic that may be gained from the various narratives about Yitzchak, whose lifestyle most closely resembles the removed existence of the scholar. A careful analysis of Yitzchak's life may yield certain clues as to the various approaches toward religious isolation and devotional study sanctioned by the Torah. More practically, we may gain guidance as to who should follow which approach.

Ivory Towers

For most readers, there is a certain lack of clarity concerning Yitzchak's rather puzzling identity. He is clearly different from Avraham and Yaakov in ways that very subtly show a unique approach to life. As opposed to the other patriarchs, Yitzchak never seems to be at the center of the narrative. Even at the pinnacle of his life – being offered as a sacrifice – Yitzchak stays in the background. Likewise, when he marries Rivka, his role still remains limited. This pattern continues throughout the rest of his adult life, which we see described in Parashat Toldot. In the few scenes where Yitzchak is actually the protagonist, he seems to limit himself to two rather conservative ways of dealing with the world: 1) to wait for events to happen to him and only then to react (e.g., when children were not granted to him and Rivka, when he is confronted by Avimelech, when Rivka tells him that he should send Yaakov away, etc.) and 2) whenever possible, to rely on the previous strategies of his father Avraham (e.g., proclaiming his wife to be his sister, making a pact with the local leader, etc.).[1]

Moreover, when it comes to basic physical needs and survival, Yitzchak simply does not seem to expend a great amount of energy. For example, the famous Renaissance-era Italian commentator R. Ovadia Seforno observes that Yitzchak allowed his sons to reach the very mature age of forty without taking an interest in their marital plans or lack thereof[2] – in startling contrast to Avraham's detailed concern for finding a spouse for Yitzchak. While his father was very concerned with marriage, Yitzchak himself was also curiously absent in the selection of his own wife.[3] Yitzchak, then, with regard to himself or to his sons, does

---

[1] See Rabbenu Bachya on *Bereshit* 26:15 for a discussion of this point.

[2] Seforno, *Bereshit* 26:34.

[3] An alternative explanation for this can be based on our suggestion of the strained relationship between Avraham and Yitzchak (see Chapter 2, p. 45, note 5). While

not seem to be particularly preoccupied with the concept of marriage at all.

Yitzchak's attitude toward the world is also highlighted by comparing his manner of dealing with human conflict with that of Avraham and Yaakov. In the parallel stories of Avraham and Yitzchak's conflict with the Philistines over the control of wells dug by their respective retinues, Avraham does not shy away from rebuking Avimelech over the matter.[4] In contrast, it seems fair to infer that Yitzchak relies on the hope that eventually God will step in, and he therefore directs his followers to keep digging wells until eventually the local inhabitants leave them alone.[5] While Yitzchak does question Avimelech about his people's attitude toward him, the question is more of a clarification than a rebuke.[6] Indeed, not only does Yitzchak not mention the conflict over the wells, he does not even mention the fact that Avimelech has previously expelled him from his territory. It appears that Yitzchak is not interested in bringing up such matters and views redress of such issues as unnecessary.

Similarly, when challenged by Avimelech about his plot to conceal his wife's true identity, Yitzchak is basically silent except to say that he was scared for his life:[7] He saw no need to use this as an

---

such an explanation could explain Avraham's reticence to involve Yitzchak in the process, it fails to explain Yitzchak's complete passivity in the whole affair. Moreover, the explanation here in this chapter fits into a clear pattern that runs through many of Yitzchak's interactions with the mundane world. A third explanation that might be offered is that God apparently did not want Yitzchak to leave Eretz Yisrael. This, however, does not appear to be the reason for his not going, as the text seems to indicate that Yitzchak himself was not aware of this proscription until later (*Bereshit* 26:2–3).

[4] *Bereshit* 21:25.

[5] Ibid., 26:18–22.

[6] Ibid., 26:27.

[7] Ibid., 26:9.

opportunity to engage Avimelech in a protracted discussion about ethics. In contrast, Avraham, being much more interested in the spiritual education of others, makes sure to explain that he felt compelled to conceal his wife's true identity because of the low moral level of the Philistines.[8] Avraham also explains the linguistic justification of calling Sarah his sister to make sure that Avimelech understands Avraham's own punctilious concern with ethics – even though from a normative halachic perspective, Avraham would certainly have been allowed to lie in order to save his life. Avraham wanted to make a point about Avimelech and his followers' need to grow religiously. From Yitzchak's very limited response, however, we see that such a point did not appear to be part of his agenda. Yitzchak's focus simply did not lay in his interactions with others.

Although Yaakov does not go through a parallel episode with Avimelech, he does encounter his own conflicts throughout his life. Yaakov first follows the non-confrontational approach of his father, only to shift to the more direct approach of his grandfather later on. With the exception of a short-lived protest to Lavan's swindle when he gives Yaakov the wrong wife, Yaakov takes his father's approach in the house of Lavan by taking much abuse without directly confronting his father-in-law. He prefers to run away from Lavan rather than directly state his claims against him. It is only after Lavan gives chase and confronts Yaakov with all sorts of claims that Yaakov finally responds in a bold and forthright fashion, showing Avraham-like concern that his own actions are seen in a proper light by others. This is largely a turning point for Yaakov. Even though, at times, he continues to exhibit indifference to poor treatment from others, he no longer does this in blanket fashion as he did in the house of Lavan. Thus, while Yaakov is clearly influenced by

---

[8] Ibid., 20:11–12.

his father's approach to the world, it becomes an approach that he largely sheds as he has more and more contact with the world around him.[9]

From this point of view, we can perhaps better appreciate Esav's involvement with his father's food.[10] Esav's passion for physical pleasure stands in marked contrast to his father's lack of concern with such matters. The special relationship between Esav and Yitzchak is characterized by Esav offering his father what he feels Yitzchak was lacking. While Yitzchak himself likely does not care much about what he eats, asking Esav to prepare food for him shows that he appreciates the show of concern by Esav in the only way that this son knows how to show it. In this way, Esav is able to offer something to Yitzchak which the young Yaakov, whose lifestyle and values most mirrored those of his father, could not.

Understanding Yitzchak as someone removed from the world can also help us understand a seemingly shocking, though quite likely, understanding of the text, wherein Yitzchak and Rivka appear to have marital relations in front of an open window.[11] We are not told exactly what Avimelech saw through the window, yet we are told that it made him understand that Yitzchak and Rivka were really husband and wife and not brother and sister as he was previously told. That he saw them involved in physical relations clearly seems to be suggested by the Midrash[12] and subsequently endorsed by Rashi.[13] Understandably, many of the commentaries on the Midrash and on Rashi[14] try to explain that this is not really what transpired. Nonetheless, if we understand that Yitzchak was never really focused on matters pertaining to this world, the

---

9 For a more complete discussion of this transformation, see Chapter 5, p. 89 ff.

10 This is the simple meaning of *Bereshit* 25:27. See also *Ha'amek Davar ad loc.*

11 *Bereshit* 26:8–9.

12 *Bereshit Rabba* 64:5.

13 Rashi, *Bereshit* 26:8.

14 Mizrachi, Levush haOrah, *et al.*

Midrash's reading of this story makes sense. Just as Yitzchak doesn't pay attention to other details of his physical existence, so too when it comes to conjugal relations he is not completely focused.

One might object to Yitzchak's lack of awareness as dangerous: By not taking a proactive and engaged approach to the world, one would expect that Yitzchak would not fare very well – especially from his vulnerable position as a stranger in the land. Yet surprisingly, even as Yitzchak does not devote much energy to his physical well-being, the world seems to treat him with kid gloves (his near-sacrifice on the altar notwithstanding). Divine providence keeps Yitzchak from enduring his father's and his son's worst experiences. When in the same situation as his father (i.e., with Avimelech), Yitzchak does not have his wife taken away from him. When Yitzchak thinks of going down to Egypt, God appears to him to prevent him from doing so, telling him that there is no need for him to go into exile.[15] In contrast, when Yaakov contemplates going to Egypt, God appears to him and tells him that he can go.[16] Finally, as opposed to both his father and his son, circumstances do not lead to Yitzchak's marrying more than one woman, which created major difficulties for both Avraham and Yaakov. Strangely enough, God not only allows for, but seems to encourage, Yitzchak's lack of interest in the world. As a result, even without possessing the worldly cleverness and engagement of Avraham and Yaakov, Yitzchak comes out of difficult predicaments smelling like a rose.

Adventuresome Spirituality

The three places where we do see innovative behavior on the part of Yitzchak all have to do with spirituality. Yitzchak is the first to clearly

---

[15] *Bereshit* 26:2–3.

[16] Ibid., 46:3–4.

pray that he be granted children. This innovation is more visibly demonstrated by carefully contrasting it to Avraham's complaint in a similar situation.[17] Avraham tells God that since he has not been able to have children, all of the blessings he received are for naught. This sounds as if there is nothing that can be done about it; thus, it is only rhetorically that Avraham asks God, "What can You give me?" This is not to say that Avraham was shortsighted in his understanding of God's ability to change the matter – there could have been many reasons for Avraham to be hesitant to ask for such a major miracle. Still, it is significant that Yitzchak overcomes the reticence of his father. As opposed to Avraham's relative passivity concerning his and his wife's infertility, Yitzchak beseeches God to redress the situation by giving him and Rivka a child.[18]

Yitzchak is innovative for a second time when he is "*suach ba-sadeh*," which is traditionally understood to mean that he was praying in the field.[19] While others had prayed before him, the demonstrative prayer in the open field seems to have taken prayer to new heights.

Yitzchak's other, even greater novelty is his decision to bless Esav. This is, in fact, the first time we hear of a human being having the "audacity" to bless another human being – a seemingly very bold move for such a conservative character, especially in view of the unlikely recipient of Divine favor. Such a stance shows us that Yitzchak was quite confident in his ability to have an impact on the Divine will. Moreover, these three examples clearly contrast Yitzchak's marked passivity in the

---

[17] Ibid., 15:2–3.

[18] Although the reader could point out that Yitzchak was able to benefit from the knowledge that God was willing to perform miracles of this type, as He had with Yitzchak's own birth, this in no way showed that prayer would be an effective way to bring about a miracle of this nature.

[19] *Berachot* 26b. This is understood to be the literal meaning of the verse by many commentators. See Malbim, S.D. Luzzatto, Y.S. Reggio, *et al.* on *Bereshit* 24:63.

physical world on the one hand and his clear willingness to pursue spiritual innovation on the other.[20]

One could see Yitzchak's differing approaches to the spiritual and the physical as two sides of the same coin. It is precisely his overriding focus on spirituality that prevented him from expending much energy on what he perceived to be the comparatively minor goings-on of the world around him. These were not only limited to purely mundane matters of food and shelter and the like, but – especially compared to Avraham – also to the spiritual edification of others. Apparently, when given a chance to be involved either with God or with his fellow human beings, Yitzchak understandably saw the latter as a relative waste of time. On some level then, by Yitzchak choosing a focus, it was only natural that other things retreated into the background.[21]

In short, we could say that Yitzchak led an ivory-tower spiritual existence. Such a view helps answer a major question asked by Ramban: Why did Rivka have to deceive Yitzchak rather than explain to him the correctness of blessing Yaakov and not Esav? The implicit basis for this question was later elaborated on by the famous nineteenth century Rosh Yeshiva, Netziv (Rabbi Naftali Tzvi Yehudah Berlin). He says that Rivka behaves completely differently from the other mothers (i.e., Sarah and Rachel) when they disagreed with their husbands' actions. We see that the other mothers felt it their prerogative to challenge their husbands' views on a number of occasions.[22] When we consider Yitzchak's unique character, however, a likely reason for Rivka's equally unique behavior emerges: it could be that she sought to preserve Yitzchak's ivory-tower

---

[20] Noach's words to his children (*Bereshit* 9:25–27) certainly include a curse, but if there is a blessing at all, it is completely reactive to a specific incident and not a general blessing meant to transmit bounty, as was the case with Yitzchak's blessing of his two sons.

[21] On the topic of the necessity of forgoing important values as a result of our choices, see Chapter 1.

[22] Most pointedly in *Bereshit* 16:5, 21:10 and 30:1.

existence, an existence he did not share with Avraham or Yaakov. Rivka thus wanted to shelter him from the more sordid facts about their son Esav.[23] In this, she seems to emulate God Himself Who, as explained earlier, also sheltered Yitzchak from too much exposure to the difficulties of life. While it was important to Rivka that Esav not get the blessing, she orchestrated it in such a way as to keep Yitzchak innocent and pure. Indeed, the rabbis refer to Yitzchak as an *olah temimah* – a pure (unblemished) sacrifice. This purity is invoked as the reason he could not go outside of Eretz Yisrael,[24] and presumably it is also this purity that Rivka was trying to protect.

An Alternative Paradigm

Yitzchak's weltanschauung represents somewhat of an anomaly in the lives of the patriarchs. It does not resemble the worldly spirituality of either Avraham and Sarah, or Yaakov and his family. Neither does it reflect the normative path of halacha, which guides the Jew through active involvement in the mundane world.

It can be said that praying during the day (*mincha*), an innovation attributed by the rabbis to Yitzchak,[25] was symbolic of his entire existence. The other prayer times, morning and night, which are associated with Avraham and Yaakov respectively, fit more naturally with the daily routine of a man of the world; he leaves his home in the morning to go into the world until evening when he returns. Yitzchak was never fully in the world and he could therefore pray while most other men were still working. No matter the time or the place, Yitzchak's entire being was focused on the spiritual.

---

[23] See *Ha'amek Davar, Bereshit* 27:46.

[24] *Bereshit Raba* 54:3.

[25] *Berachot* 26b.

Although Yitzchak was an iconoclast, there is no doubt that his personal development contributed a great deal to the foundation of the Jewish people. For one, his ivory-tower existence would serve as a model for many other great Jews later on in history. These outstanding people would likely not have found their proper path without Yitzchak's example.

Of course, even as halacha seems to advocate involvement in the world, further analysis shows that Judaism actually articulates two tracks. The first track is for the vast majority: Like Avraham and Yaakov, most people need to sacrifice some of their spiritual pursuits to bring God's presence into the world. We must show the world the beauty and harmony of a divinely inspired life and thereby fulfill our role as a "nation of priests." We can only show this to the world, however, if we live in it.[26]

But there is a second track as well. Like Yitzchak, there are some Jews whose religious genius is so great that they cannot spare any of their time to fulfill the priestly role of religious leadership for the rest of the world. Their lot is one of complete spiritual dedication. The Gaon of Vilna was such a person. It is told that when his sister came to visit him after many years of separation, he told her that he had no time to speak with her. In truth, he had no time. His time had to be solely dedicated to the development of his religious genius. He understood that his personal responsibility to the Jewish people was to develop that genius.

This unusual second track even finds its place in halacha. When the Talmudic sage Ben Azai chose not to marry because of his overwhelming devotion to Torah study, it would appear to have been against the halacha.[27] After all, Jewish men are required to marry and have children; Judaism is critical of monastic celibacy. The first halacha in the *Shulchan Arukh*'s Even haEzer section tells us that someone who does not

---

[26] See Chapter 5, especially the last section, for a discussion of the philosophy of halacha toward engagement with the world.

[27] *Yevamot* 63b.

get married and have children is considered like a murderer. However, three paragraphs later we read that someone like Ben Azai, who did not get married because of his total dedication to Torah study, is not considered a sinner. Apparently, there is halacha for most of us, which tells us how to bring Godliness into the world; and there is halacha for those who bring themselves to Godliness. This was Ben Azai, the Vilna Gaon, and the progenitor of it all, our father Yitzchak.

On some level, the primary track of Avraham and Yaakov remains superior. That is to say, it is more effective in the short term. All of Yaakov's children came out properly, which is not the case with the children of Yitzchak. While there were certainly other reasons for this outcome, it is often a natural consequence of a father's total dedication to spirituality that a child will not get the much-needed parental attention to develop properly. Similarly, we know that the more worldly approach of Rabbi Yishmael, who advocated that his students earn a livelihood, was more successful than the more rarefied approach of Rabbi Shimon bar Yochai, who told his students to let God worry about their livelihood and be involved solely with Torah study.[28] Nonetheless, God's apparent facilitation of Yitzchak's lifestyle[29] teaches us that we must allow for a second track as well. This alternative track is necessary to allow the true religious genius to make the short-term sacrifices needed to bring about his unique contribution to the long-term success of the Jewish nation. In this, as in other realms, we have to acknowledge different roles for different people within God's holy nation.

Knowing whether one has a Yitzchak personality or not is tremendously important in deciding upon his path in life. Yitzchaks

---

[28] *Berachot* 35b.

[29] It is interesting to note that R. Shimon bar Yochai was also able to have his minimal physical needs met by way of Divine intervention (i.e., during the thirteen years he spent in the cave), reiterating the contention that someone whose complete focus is on spiritual matters will often get Divine aid in taking care of his physical needs.

should certainly not be wasted. At the same time, however, for a person to pretend to have genius when he does not is also counterproductive. Indeed, Judaism's critique of asceticism is largely directed to that person. Similarly, it is to the person who would make such a mistake that the Talmud's above-mentioned story about the followers of Rabbi Shimon bar Yochai – and its implied warning – is directed. If a person is not predisposed to complete spiritual dedication, such an approach will backfire. That doesn't mean that the approach is not legitimate; it certainly worked for Rabbi Shimon himself. Rather, the Talmud is telling us that ivory-tower spirituality will backfire for the vast majority of people who lack the religious genius of a Rabbi Shimon or our father Yitzchak.

CHAPTER 5

Redeeming Our Civilization: Yaakov and Esav Revisited

Brotherhood of Jew and Gentile

Since many of us work and/or live in the general gentile culture, we experience a certain cognitive dissonance between the many pleasant, intelligent and morally upstanding non-Jews we know and the negative stereotype we think normative Jewish tradition casts upon the non-Jew. To use my own personal experience as an example, some of the most religious people I know are not Jewish. Anyone who has lived among devout Christians will likely echo these sentiments.

When we try to reconcile what we see around us with what we believe is in our tradition, we are often at a loss. We come to a dangerous situation where we are forced to ask ourselves the question made famous by Chico Marx: "Who you gonna believe, me or your own eyes?" Seeking out positive paradigms of Jewish-gentile interaction in the Jewish tradition has tremendous practical ramifications. Of course, if such paradigms do not exist, it would be dishonest to pretend otherwise, no matter how desirable such paradigms might be. Upon deeper investigation, however, we shall see that not only do they exist, but they may in fact represent a major undercurrent in the traditional Jewish weltanshauung.

It is certainly true that there are many rabbinic statements that seem to cast a very negative light on non-Jews. We will not discuss the very attractive possibility made famous by the great medieval Talmudic scholar, R. Menachem haMeiri, that the Talmud was dealing with a morally delinquent type of non-Jew that we generally do not encounter today.[1] Rather, we will focus on many other, less known statements in the Talmud that shed a different light on Jewish attitudes toward the non-Jew. While the rabbis were certainly disappointed by the low moral standards of the gentile society around them, we will see that their disappointment coexisted with a clear recognition of the non-Jew's potential to become our partners in creating a better world.

The Biblical narrative of the relationship between Yaakov and Esav, who are depicted in post-Biblical Jewish literature as the prototypical Jew and gentile respectively, is the most fertile story for understanding the Jewish approach to the non-Jew. In spite of the animosity the rabbis may have had for the pagan societies around them, they could not help but notice the nuanced way in which the Torah treats the relationship between the two brothers. It is a complex relationship, wherein Yaakov is not always the hero and Esav not always the villain. Moreover, it is no coincidence that our Biblical commentators (parshanim) have long seen this section as a paradigm for how we are to interact with the gentiles, and with the Christian nations in particular.[2]

Indeed, Rabbi Samson Raphael Hirsch seems to view the reunion of the two brothers as foreshadowing the positive developments of his own time.[3] His Eastern European contemporary, Rabbi Naftali Tzvi

---

[1] See *Beit haBechira* on *Baba Kama* 37b, one of the many places where he mentions this idea. See also the author's article, "Religious Censorship in the Information Age – Libertarian Implications of Contemporary Realia," archived at www.cardozoschool.org.

[2] See Ramban and the summation of Abarbanel on the first section of *Bereshit*, Chap. 33. These commentators take their cue from the Talmudic sages themselves, who would often look into this section of the Torah before making decisions concerning how to deal with the Roman authorities (*Bereshit Rabba* 78:15).

[3] See his commentary on *Bereshit* 33:4, 10–11.

Yehudah Berlin (Netziv), also strikes an optimistic tone regarding the Jewish people's willingness to seek brotherhood with the spiritual descendants of Esav given the proper circumstances.[4] Both of these commentators present modern insights, and both concentrate on what Esav has to do to bring about rapprochement. In this chapter, we will analyze the flip side of this modern rapprochement – that which is incumbent upon Yaakov.

Particularly instructive is the opening narrative of Parashat Vayishlach, which recounts the dramatic reunion of Yitzchak's two sons. Yaakov's fear and apprehension give way to cautious relief as his brother is successfully appeased – Esav seems to cave in to brotherly sentiment toward the very same Yaakov he had previously marked for bloody vengeance. Such a positive reversal is well worth investigating. What happened to change Esav's attitude toward his brother? In order to answer this question, we need to analyze the respective development of the prototypical brothers.

Of Names and Transformations

While the Torah's narratives of Yaakov and Esav show much character development, there are some fundamental differences. Of central importance is the changing of Yaakov's name to Yisrael. Name changes are significant, as they signify a change of identity.[5] The change here is especially meaningful since it is a complete change as opposed to a mere emendation, as with Avram becoming AvraHam or Hoshea becoming YEhoshua. Esav, for his part, takes on the name of Edom, but this cannot be construed as indicative of any real transformation of identity

---

[4] *Ha'amek Davar, Bereshit* 33:4.

[5] See Prof. Yeshayahu Liebowitz, *Accepting the Yoke of Heaven: Commentary on the Weekly Torah Portion* (New York & Jerusalem: Urim Publications, 2006) pp. 38–39.

because the Torah never again calls him by this relatively casual nickname. From this point of view, Esav's multi-faceted personality notwithstanding, he remains a static character compared to his twin brother Yaakov, who goes through a major transformation.

Esav

There is a major current in Midrash that understands Esav's display of affection upon his reunion with Yaakov to be insincere. Nonetheless, most major commentators follow the midrashic opinion that accepts Esav's behavior at face value, following the simple meaning of the text.[6] Along with Rav Shimon bar Elazar,[7] these commentators sense that Esav feels true compassion for the brother he had once sworn to murder. Yet, as indicated by the lack of a name change, Esav doesn't fundamentally change. That being the case, we must try to understand further what brought about such a radical shift in Esav.

It is likely that the very real transformation in *Yaakov's* character engenders a new *response* from his brother. This understanding of Esav's change of heart dovetails the widely held view that Esav originally brought a war party to attack Yaakov upon his long-delayed return home to Israel.[8] According to this approach, the change of heart occurs in Esav sometime between Esav's going out to confront Yaakov and their actual meeting. Most likely, the wealth and political savvy behind the sophisticated retinue of gifts sent by Yaakov creates doubts in Esav's mind. Although Esav came with hostile intentions, the gifts do not fit in to the picture he had of Yaakov based on the last time he had contact with him. Yaakov's unexpected approach forces Esav to reevaluate his

---

[6] See, for example, Rashi, Abarbanel, Seforno, Malbim, and especially Rabbi S.R. Hirsch and *Ha'amek Davar*.

[7] *Bereshit Rabba* 78:9.

[8] See Bachya, Seforno *et al.* on *Bereshit* 32:7.

position toward his brother. Thus, by the time Esav actually meets Yaakov, he understands that it is no longer Yaakov whom he meets, but rather Yisrael. Consequently, it is his "new" brother who is able to elicit a change in Esav's hostile stance.

Yaakov

Yaakov is introduced in the Torah as being "*tam*" and sitting in tents. The latter is traditionally understood to describe a studious and meditative character.[9] The word *tam* generally conveys purity and innocence, as when it describes an unblemished offering (e.g., a *keves tamim*). Rashi elucidates the trait of being *tam* by contrasting it with Esav's character: Whereas Esav wields an expertise in the ways of deceit, the words out of Yaakov's mouth innocently convey his true feelings.[10] While such honesty is certainly admirable, in an imperfect world it can leave one most vulnerable. An amusing example of this is when Yaakov admonishes a group of ostensibly lazing shepherds for not working.[11] To put it into a modern-day context, envision a truck stop, where truck drivers are lazily stretching out their meal. In comes a yeshiva student asking the group why they don't get back to work, since it is obvious they would not want to cheat their employers. Clearly, the student would require Divine protection to prevent him from making it onto the next morning's obituary list.

The above example seems to indicate that Yaakov always felt it appropriate to speak the truth. If anything, his one prior experience with deception – when his mother commanded him to deceive his father in order to get the blessing intended for Esav – may well have left him

---

[9] See *Bereshit Rabba* 63:10.

[10] Rashi, *Bereshit* 25:27.

[11] *Bereshit* 29:7. But see, for example, Rashi and Seforno as to the nature of Yaakov's criticism.

convinced that honesty is always the best policy. In contrast, the rabbis point out that telling the truth is not appropriate in every situation. As mentioned in Chapter 2, truth does not always outweigh other values.

Alongside Yaakov's sheltered approach to morality is a sheltered approach to the material world. Having no wife or children and presumably focused solely on cerebral interests, Yaakov's meager physical needs were easily addressed by his father's apparently ample means. In fact, his parents' home sheltered him from needing to deal with the imperfections of the world. Like his father Yitzchak,[12] Yaakov could devote all of his time to developing his own spiritual world. In short, while living with his parents, Yaakov lived an ivory-tower existence.

In Lavan's house, Yaakov comes of age. Arriving with few physical possessions, he is forced to work for Lavan in order to earn his keep. Thus, his pursuit of spirituality to the exclusion of marriage, family and financial pursuits comes to an end. Following seven years of work for Lavan, Yaakov finally gets married to no less than four women in quick succession.

Marriage in and of itself brings about an understanding of competing values. Quite obviously, no matter how good the marriage, two different people will always have some conflicting needs. Negotiating these inevitable conflicts is an unavoidable part of sharing one's life. If adjusting to the challenges of married life is difficult for the average person, it is easy to imagine how taxing it must have been for Yaakov to try to create marital harmony with all four of his wives.

Moreover, having to provide for the needs of his family forces Yaakov to deal with the pressures of the working world. The desire to earn a proper living tempts many people to take moral shortcuts, in order to get a "better deal." In the house of Lavan, taking these shortcuts was

---

[12] See Chapter 4, as well as R. Adin Steinsaltz's essay on Yitzchak in *Biblical Images* (New York: Basic Books, 1984) pp. 31–40.

likely the rule rather than the exception, and Yaakov had to exert great energy to maintain his moral code.[13]

Realizing Yaakov's initial innocence, Lavan exploits the "opportunity" by employing deceit in every aspect of their relationship. Thus, Yaakov complains that Lavan changes his terms of employment whenever it suits the latter's advantage.[14] The most famous change occurs when Lavan substitutes Leah for Rachel, forcing Yaakov to work twice as long as originally agreed in order to marry the woman promised him. No doubt, Yaakov had very little experience with this sort of deception before he left Yitzchak's house.

In short, Yaakov is abruptly thrown into very trying circumstances. He learns that life outside of the "yeshiva" is not a moral utopia. It is less pristine and much more complex. In Lavan's house Yaakov learns to deal with deceit, domestic friction and material exigencies – in other words, he learns how to apply his spiritual lessons and beliefs to what we call the "real world." While the details of Yaakov's adaptation process are not so clear, we do gain great insight about such a process by the transformation that we see in Yaakov upon his return back to his ancestral homeland.

As Yaakov prepares to meet Esav, he has a galvanizing experience that confirms his transformation and makes him into a new man worthy of a new name. As the Torah documents, Yaakov leaves Lavan's house with ample possessions he earned there. His reunion with Yitzchak could bring about the beginning of a business dynasty. Yet perhaps this gave Yaakov reason to pause. Upon his return, he has to decide how far he wants to pursue his material potential at the expense of spiritual endeavor.

---

[13] See Rashi on *Bereshit* 32:5. This is probably what Rashi alludes to when indicating that Yaakov celebrated his ability to maintain his religious observance while in Lavan's house.

[14] *Bereshit* 31:41.

This is precisely how R. Shlomo Ephraim of Lontshitz (Kli Yakar) understands the rabbinic traditions which explain that Yaakov backtracked across the Yabok River in order to collect small jars left behind[15] – only to be accosted by the spiritual forces of Esav.[16] With this act, claims Kli Yakar, Yaakov shows a dangerous weakness for property: he had no business risking his life to salvage such an obviously insignificant portion of his wealth.[17] While neither the Torah nor the Midrash reveals exactly what occurred during Yaakov's struggle with the mysterious "man," the context of Yaakov's personal journey outlined above gives strong support to Kli Yakar's understanding of the text.

Thus, according to Kli Yakar, we can more clearly understand why Yaakov is fighting the forces of Esav specifically at this time: As a man of means, Yaakov can turn into another Esav – ruled by his desire for physical gratification. The other option is to overcome this drive and become what is known as "Yisrael." Yisrael is the one who can enjoy the physical world within the proper parameters and therefore be in control of his desires. In fact, the very name Yisrael is indicative of a newly found "*srara*," or dominion. Moreover, if the reference to his dominion over "*elohim*" is understood to refer to the materialistic tendencies embodied by Esav as per Kli Yakar, then we have good reason to believe that Yaakov's personality transformation has much to do with his attitude toward physical comfort and pleasure. This is the essence of what the rabbis deem to be the struggle with the spiritual forces of Esav. Once Yaakov has created his own paradigm for thriving spiritually within the

---

[15] *Chulin* 91a.

[16] *Bereshit Rabba* 77:3.

[17] Kli Yakar on *Bereshit* 2:25. The rabbis (*Chulin* 91a) seemingly justify Yaakov's behavior by appending the dictum, "Beloved are the possessions of the righteous." Yet it is questionable whether this is meant to condone Yaakov's behavior in view of the danger to his life, which the Talmud points out immediately after the above statement.

physical world as Yisrael, he will be greeted by Esav in an entirely new light.

Potential Symbiosis

The rabbis indicate that it is not only Yaakov who is interested in matters of the spirit, but also Esav. The Midrash tells us that in their mother's womb, the brothers are fighting for *both* worlds.[18] If Esav were only interested in this world, there would be no contest about the next world (i.e., spirituality). While Esav is not willing to give up this world in order to get a ticket into the next world, this does not mean that he is automatically ready to forget about spiritual pursuits.

It is in the context of the transformed Yaakov (i.e., Yisrael) that Netziv reminds us of the potentially symbiotic relationship that can exist between the descendants of Yaakov and the descendants of Esav, specifically embodied by Rabbi Yehudah haNasi (Rebbi) and Antoninus.[19] The spiritual greatness of Rebbi was used to elevate Antoninus, while in turn Antoninus could provide for Rebbi's temporal needs.[20] When the latter taught the former, the power and splendor of Rome was placed at the disposal of the Jewish leader. Seforno suggests that this potential symbiotic relationship was what was envisioned by Yitzchak when he wanted to bless Esav with physical wealth and power.[21]

---

[18] *Avoda Zara* 11a.

[19] *Ha'amek Davar, Bereshit* 32:25.

[20] See *Avoda Zara* 10b.

[21] Seforno on *Bereshit* 27:29. Although Yitzchak is generally viewed as having made a mistake in wanting to apply this potential to Esav himself, the plain text is somewhat unclear. One wonders about what would have happened had Yitzchak given the blessings as planned. Moreover, in *Bereshit Rabba* 76:9, the Midrash blames Yaakov for not allowing Esav the opportunity to repent. In fact, based on this midrash, the author of *Torah Temimah* (*Bereshit* 32, end of note 9) feels forced to say

Yaakov's worldview (as opposed to Yisrael's) did not allow for the symbiotic relationship of Rebbi and Antoninus. Judging by Yaakov's earlier pursuits, he seems to view spirituality as something that excludes physical and mundane interests. This helps explain why Yaakov feels justified in coercing his brother into giving him the birthright. According to Rashi, the birthright coveted by Yaakov was not the double portion of inheritance, but rather the duties of being the family priest that were customarily entrusted to the firstborn. Following this understanding of Yaakov buying the birthright from Esav, we see that Yaakov cannot fathom any spiritual greatness coming from someone like his brother.[22] In Yaakov's worldview, where one must choose between spirituality and physicality, Esav's choice of physicality over spirituality axiomatically disqualifies him from the spiritual benefits offered by the birthright. As such, there is no room for cooperation or symbiosis. Lacking any room for dialogue, Yaakov is left with no alternative but to manipulate and coerce his brother in order to acquire the spiritual opportunities given by the birthright – opportunities he believes could benefit only him and not his worldly brother.

For most of humanity, Yaakov's all-or-nothing approach is not an attractive paradigm. For one, it requires an uncommon level of discipline and motivation. Furthermore, it is insulting to mankind's very nature, which pushes one in the direction of physical pleasure. Thus, a "Yaakov" approach shuts out anyone not willing or able to shun the physical.

When religion is presented as choosing between this world and the next, it can easily breed resentment and anger. Moreover, a religious

---

that Yaakov *knew* that Esav would actually repent if he would have married Dina; otherwise, how can Yaakov be blamed for preventing Esav from meeting her? According to this, it is not clear whether Yitzhak was more blind in the short term than was Rivka in the long term.

[22] Rashi, *Bereshit* 25:31, based on *Bereshit Rabba* 63:13, posits that Yaakov's motivation in wanting the birthright was to prevent Esav from offering sacrifices to God, something for which he felt Esav was totally inappropriate.

formula that can only maintain itself when divorced from the physical is seen as intrinsically flawed. The fact that it cannot work outside the ivory tower proves its inadequacy. Christian monastic tradition can be viewed as an extension of Yaakov's proposition. Ultimately then, Esav's anger may be focused more on that which *Yaakov* represents than on Yaakov himself.

Yisrael, as opposed to Yaakov, represents an entirely different proposition, one embodied by normative Judaism. According to this approach, the physical is endorsed. When placed in the context of ultimate spiritual goals, sensual pleasures are sanctioned as long as they are kept in check.

The paradigm of Yisrael is the *only* possibility for the spiritual descendants of Esav. When the Jews display such a model, it can be appreciated by humanity at large. Its accessibility allows the average person to pursue his yearning for God, a yearning that exists in everyone. It is not coincidental that the paradigm of symbiosis is the relationship between Rebbi and Antoninus, as Rebbi was a Yisrael personality. The Talmud compares the lavishness of his banquets to that of his royal Roman interlocutor.[23] Thus, Rebbi was known for his wealth and power as well as for his scholarship. As such, he was an attractive figure for the spiritually keen descendent of Esav.

On some level, it may be more difficult to succeed as a Yisrael than a Yaakov: Yaakov fights temptation by avoiding contact with it, whereas Yisrael confronts and fights it directly. To be a Yisrael requires constant vigilance. Yet halacha is largely made up of such vigilance. For example, rather than putting severe ascetic limits on our diet, halacha provides a spiritual framework around it. It does this through the

---

[23] *Avoda Zara* 11a. Although the same Talmud (*Ketubot* 104a) tells us that Rebbi became ascetic in several respects, there can be no doubt that as *Nasi* he continued to be actively involved in worldly affairs.

requirement to invoke God before and after eating and drinking.[24] Likewise, if we are to understand Yaakov-Yisrael as a model for continued growth, it would follow that Yisrael represents a higher level of development, as Yaakov ultimately becomes Yisrael.[25]

Contemporary Corollaries

In line with our Introduction, one hesitates to suggest contemporary conclusions for fear of imposing ideas that do not necessarily follow from the above analysis. Nevertheless, three modest notions do seem in order:

1) On the individual level, there is an organic process that can take one from being a Yaakov to becoming a Yisrael. In other words, being Yaakov is usually a necessary step if we are to eventually become Yisrael. While emulating the worldly Yisrael should be our goal, we can only achieve that goal if we prepare for it by building ourselves in a Yaakov-like atmosphere free of major challenges. Thus, the benefits of exposing

---

[24] An excellent example of this approach in halacha is the dictum of R. Yehoshua that holidays should be celebrated by physical enjoyment as well as spiritual pursuits (*Beitza* 15b and *Pesachim* 68b). In this, he opposes the approach of R. Eliezer, which favors total immersion in spiritual pursuits. While their reasoning is based on textual proofs and the halacha is decided in favor of R. Yehoshua on technical grounds (see Meiri on *Pesachim*, ibid.), we can see R. Yehoshua's teaching as a reflection of the Yisrael approach, whereas R. Eliezer reflects the Yaakov approach. Both have validity and are therefore to be found latent in the text, but R. Yehoshua's view is generally accepted over R. Eliezer's, since his represents a more mainstream halachic tradition.

[25] Yaakov-Yisrael represents the model that is appropriate for the Jewish people as a whole, especially in their role as a nation of priests. This is not to deny the need for certain individuals to follow a different model, however, as described in the previous chapter.

our children to the outside world and its challenges before the children are properly formed are outweighed by the long-term disadvantages. Yaakov applies to the real world what he learned in the ivory-tower existence of his youth, without compromising. It is unlikely that he would have gained this inner strength without solid immersion in ethical and spiritual preparation throughout his formative years.

Indeed, Yaakov applies this lesson concerning his own children, rebuffing a friendly Esav's offer to help and protect him, by telling him that the children are "soft."[26] Ostensibly, he is telling Esav that his children cannot keep up with the strenuous pace of Esav's camp. Yet within his words, one can find an allusion to an important lesson that Yaakov learns from his own life: His children are not just tender physically. More important, they are still tender in their values and so, not yet ready to withstand the compromising influence of Esav and his band. One day, when they mature to emulate their father Yisrael, they will be resilient. In the meantime, they must remain sheltered from pernicious moral influences. Thus, while one should become a Yisrael, one cannot do so during childhood. Rather, one must first become a Yaakov, only later moving on to the next step.

2) Judaism is rooted in ancient times, when there was little common ground with the competing pagan ideologies. Consequently, denigration of any group outside of Judaism can be, and often has been, the natural continuation of our view of earlier pagan societies. While equating ancient pagan cultures with contemporary gentile cultures may be natural, it is not necessarily correct.

In fact, a nuanced reading of the rabbinic literature concerning Esav allows us to distinguish between the potential Esav and the actual

---

[26] *Bereshit* 33:13.

Esav. Indeed, some rabbinic sources point explicitly in such a direction.[27] In a larger context, the rabbis who certainly had good reason to look with disgust at the corrupted ways and beliefs of their neighbors realized that these neighbors had the potential to be otherwise. They saw that dichotomy between the Divinely implanted potential and the corrupted reality personified by the Biblical Esav. The analysis presented in this chapter is largely based on such a reading of rabbinic sources. If it is a correct reading, we certainly cannot take it for granted that the spiritual descendants of Esav will never move toward reaching their potential.[28] On the contrary, we must be prepared that their potential can be actualized.

Our analysis of Esav's reaction to both Yaakov and Yisrael highlights the former's spiritual aspirations. We have seen various traditional sources that show Esav's interest in ethical behavior and some of his descendants' interest in Torah study.[29] Rather than discounting such aspirations as ephemeral or feigned, these sources see them as something very real, to which Yaakov and his descendants may need to respond. In other words, a more nuanced reading of Jewish tradition may well indicate that we should take the religious and ethical strivings of non-Jews in the Modern period quite seriously.[30]

---

[27] See *Bereshit Rabba* 76:9, which blames Yaakov for not bringing out this potential, and *Midrash Shir haShirim Zuta* 1:13, which equates Esav's potential to that of Avraham, Yitzchak and Yaakov.

[28] Indeed, Rabbi S.R. Hirsch, in his commentary on *Bereshit* 33:4, asserts that we should expect that over time Esav will in fact come closer to such a potential.

[29] See pp. 93–94, and especially note 21.

[30] This may be obvious to many readers without the textual analysis presented in this chapter. Such a conclusion, however, is not clear from a simple perusal of rabbinic literature. Indeed, as is well-known, the vast majority of rabbinic literature presents Esav as both brutish and immoral. It is not my intention to pretend that such sources don't exist. Rather, I am suggesting a more nuanced view of these sources that is more compatible with the seemingly dissenting rabbinic sources that

3) If there is a real responsiveness to spirituality among non-Jews today, then being an educational vanguard for the nations of the world, as implied by the term "*mamlechet kohanim*," requires us to evaluate our national behavior in terms of its usefulness to mankind. While this does not necessarily supersede all other considerations, in a world of increasing international communication and awareness, we cannot understand this role as a mere nicety for pontificating to ourselves.

---

paint a more positive picture, as well as with contemporary reality. In this, I am taking a road already trailblazed by some of the great commentators of the nineteenth century such as Rabbi S. R. Hirsh (see above, note 3), Rabbi N.T.Y. Berlin (see above, note 4), and Rabbi Baruch haLevi Epstein (see above, note 2).

CHAPTER 6

Redeeming Our Ideals:
Yehudah and the Making of a Jewish Leader

Leadership can be defined as the art of getting people to do what they don't want to do. The truth is that we all find ourselves in situations where we want and even need to get others to do what we think is correct.

A very common experience of leadership, usually taken for granted, is parenthood. When we think of leadership, we often forget that parents serve as the most basic model of benign leadership.[1] After all, parents guide their children to do what their offspring don't yet realize is in their own best interest. In this role, they perform one of the most important leadership functions in any society.

Beyond our families, we are often expected to show leadership within our peer groups and our communities, even if we are not given a formal leadership position. Any responsible grouping of people expects all of its members to show leadership when needed. Thus, leadership is not at all limited to individuals who take on directorial positions in government, community or commerce. It is rather a life situation relevant to almost everyone.

Effective leadership is not just a practical matter, it is rooted in morality. The long-term success of a regime is based on the trust the constituents place in it. That trust is frequently engendered by the leader's

---

[1] See in this regard Seforno on *Bemidbar* 11:12.

respect for those whom he is leading, which in turn is often rooted in the appreciation that all people are made in the image of God. When a leader respects his followers, it also shows the central virtue of humility, which, though appropriate for all, is often lost by those who hold power. Leadership characteristics are of universal interest. Nevertheless, because proper leadership touches on morality, the Torah has a particular interest in developing paradigms that will aid in the development of such leadership.

It should come as no surprise, then, that the Torah addresses the issue of leadership early on, even before the Jewish nation enters its formative exile in Egypt. With the birth of Yaakov's twelve sons, we have the first serious contest of succession for Jewish leadership. While Yishmael and Esav both bitterly contested their respective brothers' succession, from a Jewish point of view it was really no contest. With the sons of Yaakov, however, each one was enough of a leader to be the progenitor of a semi-autonomous tribe. Yet only three of the twelve actually attempted to take on the national leadership: Reuven, Yehudah and Yosef. Reuven and Yosef's being firstborn sons notwithstanding, it is the fourth son, Yehudah, who emerges victorious. In analyzing the Torah's paradigms of proper leadership, it is worthwhile to examine the qualities that kept Yosef and Reuven back as well as those that brought Yehudah to the fore.

Effective Leadership: Reuven Surpassed

Both Reuven and Yehudah confront several situations where they have to get others to do what they otherwise wouldn't do. First, they have to convince their brothers not to kill Yosef. Second, they have to convince their father to allow them to return to Egypt with Binyamin. Finally, they have to convince Yosef to release Binyamin and allow him to go back to his father.

These three situations also correspond to the natural development of a successful leader. In order to command the respect of a larger community, one has to first develop a constituency of followers. The second stage in such a career is to rise above competitors, asserting the correctness of one's vision over those of rivals. The third step in successful leadership is to be able to assert one's will on others outside the community. In the international context, this would correspond to the influence one can exert on other nation-states. Moving through these three stages, Yehudah emerges as a model leader.

In contrast, Reuven's awkward attempts at leadership rarely meet with success. He attains a small victory in his most likely sphere of influence, among his brothers. When he attempts to move out of that circle, even slightly, to exert influence on his father, he is completely rebuffed. The consequence is for Reuven to abandon the prospect of leadership altogether. Yehudah, however, is not only able to bend the will of his brothers, he uses his remarkable early success to move on to bigger and bigger challenges as he faces first his father and then the viceroy of Egypt, his brother.

In these three situations we have a dramatic contrast between the effectiveness of Yehudah and the ineffectiveness of Reuven. It is no accident that Yehudah's natural leadership abilities are so greatly magnified by his brother Reuven's weaknesses. As in earlier situations, here too, the Torah is calling out to us to delve into its subtle messages.

Saving Yosef – Forming a Constituency

Reuven heard and he saved [Yosef] from their hand; he said, "We shall not smite a soul." Reuven said to them, "Don't spill blood, send him into this pit that is in the desert and don't send your hand upon him," so that he could save him from their hand to return him to his father…. They took him and sent him into the pit. (*Bereshit* 37:21–22, 24)

They sat to eat bread….Yehudah said to his brothers, "What is the gain if we kill our brother and cover his blood? Let us go and sell him to the Yishmaelites and let not our hand be upon him, since he is our brother, our flesh." His brothers listened. (Ibid., 37:25–27)

Reuven returned to the pit and behold, Yosef was not in the pit. [Reuven] tore his clothes. He returned to his brothers, he said, "The boy is no longer and I, where will I go?" (Ibid., 37:29–30)

Comparing Reuven's and Yehudah's respective plans to save Yosef, we notice striking differences. First, we see that Reuven tries to manipulate his brothers, whereas Yehudah works through *consensus*: Reuven tells them to throw Yosef into the pit, so that he can secretly take him out later when the rest of the brothers are not looking. Manipulative leadership is naturally problematic. Its surreptitious nature means that it is more fragile, requiring constant secrecy, lest the leader's true intentions be revealed. It also engenders distrust.

The Torah shows us the fragility of such an approach by having Reuven reappear too late, when Yosef is already gone. Whereas Reuven only obtains an uneasy concession from his brothers,[2] Yehudah is able to get his brothers' full endorsement. Rashi marks the difference between the brothers' responses to Reuven and Yehudah. He notes that the Torah writes that the brothers "listened to" Yehudah, which denotes

---

[2] See Ramban, *Bereshit* 37:22, who cites the brothers' later discussion (42:22) as proof that the Torah initially only reports Reuven's final position in his discussion with his brothers. Apparently, he had tried to convince them not to kill Yosef, but was only able to get them to compromise and, at least, not to cause his death directly.

acceptance – something absent from their earlier acquiescence to Reuven.[3]

From the beginning, Yehudah prefers to work a public and *open* compromise rather than a secret victory. Even had Reuven succeeded in saving Yosef, the deception would have certainly brought fraternal strife in its wake, which might well have brought about an even greater disaster than Yosef's going down to Egypt. Moreover, Reuven's credibility as a leader would have always been impaired. Not so Yehudah. He tells his brothers exactly what he proposes and waits for their agreement, realizing that it is the key to the creation of a positive working relationship in the future.

More than anything else, however, it is *timing* that allows Yehudah to save Yosef from the pit. While Reuven's response is immediate, Yehudah waits for his brothers to calm down and for their guilt feelings to start seeping in before he attempts to convince them. In other words, the brothers had to be ready to listen.

Granted, in this particular case, Yehudah could be blamed for not taking immediate action, as it could have cost Yosef his life. Nevertheless, Yehudah's hesitation here is mitigated – at this early stage the brothers naturally would have looked to the eldest brother, Reuven, for leadership. It would have been even presumptuous of Yehudah to upstage his older brother. Thus, in this particular case, Yehudah's timing is a luxury afforded him by Reuven, who took on his expected leadership position in the more difficult situation – when the brothers were most poised to kill Yosef. We can only speculate what Yehudah would have done had Reuven not been present.[4] Be that as it may, it should already be clear to the reader that Yehudah understood that timing is a most critical tool in bending the will of others.

---

[3] Rashi, *Bereshit* 37:27, based on *Targum Onkelos.*

[4] Yehudah later shows the ability to act immediately when it is required in saving Binyamin from imprisonment in Egypt.

Convincing the Patriarch – Taking Charge

We can also gain important insights by comparing the way Reuven and Yehudah each try to convince their father to allow them to return to Egypt with Binyamin:

> Reuven spoke to his father saying, "You can kill my two sons if I don't bring [Binyamin] to you. Let him [come] with me and I will return him to you." (*Bereshit* 42:37)
>
> And Yehudah said to Yisrael his father, "Send [Binyamin] with me and we will get up and go, so that we will live and not die, both we and you, and also our babies. I will be his guarantor. From my hand you may request him. If I don't bring him to you and present him in front of you, I will have sinned against you all the days. For had we not delayed, we would have already returned twice." (Ibid., 43:8–10)

Yaakov's indifference to Reuven's plea is easily understood, given the assurances Reuven gives his father. If Reuven's plan fails and Binyamin is lost, Yaakov is given the right to inflict suffering measure for measure (*midah k'neged midah*) on Reuven by killing the latter's own sons. It is hard to imagine why Reuven would believe that Yaakov would be motivated by the thought of killing his own grandchildren.[5] In contrast, Yehudah provides convincing arguments, personal responsibility and appeal to the unity of the group he is trying to lead. Compared to Reuven, who speaks of my children vs. your children, Yehudah speaks about the survival of all three generations together. Knowing that Yaakov cares greatly for his children as well as his grandchildren, Yehudah points out that if they don't go to Egypt, the entire nation will die. Not only does Yehudah stress his personal responsibility for Binyamin to his father, he displays a high level of credibility in his commitment to live up

---

[5] See Rashi, *Bereshit* 42:38, based on *Bereshit Rabba* 91:9.

to it. When Binyamin is arrested, it comes as no surprise that Yehudah immediately offers himself up as a captive, in place of the brother he has sworn to protect.

Another clever tactic used by Yehudah and missed by Reuven is to make it a situation of "us" and not "you and me." Yehudah convinces Yaakov that he and his father are both on the same side in their mutual predicament. When Yaakov understands that he and his son *are on the same side*, he sees the option of sending the brothers back to Egypt in a different light.

More than anything else, however, here too Yehudah is a master of timing. Reuven's idea of timing is to address a situation as soon as it arises. Yehudah knows that one must be patient, and that silence is better than speaking to men unwilling to listen. When the moment is not right, a skilled leader bides his time. As soon as the brothers return from Egypt without Shimon, Reuven tries to convince Yaakov to take the necessary risks and send them back with Binyamin. Yaakov was certainly still in shock at the loss of Shimon, a loss compounded by the earlier disappearance of Yosef, and he certainly was in no mood to take more risks. Fully aware of this, Yehudah bides his time and waits for the famine to get more pressing – he understands that eventually his father will calm down and realize the futility of his obstinacy. The Midrash in *Bereshit Rabba*[6] formalizes this into an actual discussion, wherein Yehudah tells his brothers to leave Yaakov alone and to come back to their father only when they run out of bread. Later, when they appear to be running out of food and Yaakov actually suggests that they go to Egypt to acquire more, Yehudah senses his cue to convince his father to allow Binyamin to go down with them to Egypt. Yehudah knew that the most convincing proofs would not have worked until then, when Yaakov was ready to listen.

---

[6] 91:6.

Once Yaakov is ready to listen, Yehudah uses some of the boldest speech ever heard by a son to his father in the Torah. By telling Yaakov that they could have already come back twice, Yehudah places the blame for their predicament squarely on his father. Without the right timing, such words would have been rejected out of hand. Now, however, they gain Yaakov's acquiescence.

Facing Yosef – Defeating the Adversary

One difference between the first two and the third encounters with Yosef in Egypt is the leadership dynamic of the brothers. In the first meeting (*Bereshit* 42:10–22), the brothers are always speaking as a group, with the one exception of Reuven's brief interjection of "I told you so" (verse 22) when they recognize their guilt in their earlier treatment of Yosef. In the second encounter, before Binyamin is framed, the brothers are still speaking as a group. Afterwards, when the brothers are arrested and there is a need for leadership, it is no longer Reuven who steps up but Yehudah. Now that Yehudah's leadership has come to the fore, the text (44:14) describes the group as "Yehudah, and his brothers." Yehudah now becomes the undisputed leader, to be confirmed by Yaakov later on.[7]

Rabbenu Bachya highlights Yehudah's wisdom in how he speaks to Yosef, who has just framed Binyamin. Yehudah had every right to be angry at this time. He easily could have accused Yosef of creating a conspiracy designed to give them trouble. Instead, Yehudah remains *goal-oriented*, his priority Binyamin's release.[8] Rather than argue with Yosef, Yehudah speaks to Yosef's conscience. He does this after he notices the Egyptian viceroy's curious sentimentality toward his father: After having

---

[7] See *Bereshit* 46:28, 49:8–12.

[8] Rabbenu Bachya, Introduction to Parashat Vayigash.

previously asked about Yaakov's well-being,[9] Yosef now wishes the brothers a peaceful journey and sends them back to their father.[10] Having just imprisoned Binyamin, Yosef meant to make a point that the brothers never really cared about their father's well-being – not earlier when they sold him and not now when they were about to lose Binyamin. Whether Yehudah caught Yosef's bitter irony or not, he sees the viceroy's own concern for their father as his best weapon to parry back at him.

In this interchange, Yehudah gets even more than he bargained for. Yehudah fully expects Yosef the viceroy to give in to him; yet Yosef his brother breaks down completely. The Torah states that Yosef could no longer contain himself, which means that Yosef actually intended to continue the charade even longer. Yehudah, however, knowing what to say as well as when to say it, makes Yosef understand that he is not obligated to go through with his plan to make Binyamin a slave and has the choice to do otherwise. Moreover, Yehudah's speech makes Yosef realize that he is no longer the victim, but rather has now become the victimizer. Whereas the brothers had caused grief to Yosef and Yaakov in the past, Yehudah convinces Yosef that it is now he, Yosef, who has become the new cause of the family's anguish.

Leadership and Communication

It is interesting to note that no one ever answers Reuven. In every section mentioned above, Reuven's statements are generally ignored.[11] At best, as with his suggestion to throw Yosef into the pit, his brothers silently obey. Yehudah, on the other hand, is always involved in conversations. What seems to account for this difference is that Yehudah speaks *with* people,

---

[9] *Bereshit* 43:27.

[10] Ibid., 44:17.

[11] Even when Yaakov answers Reuven (*Bereshit* 42:38), he completely ignores his suggestion.

whereas Reuven speaks at them. Indeed, effective leadership is predicated upon understanding the art of communication.

After all, speech is, first and foremost, a means of communication, which means that our words should be used to get across a message. Using words properly, however, requires forethought. The famous *mussar* personality, Rav Shlomo Wolbe *zt"l*, initiated long pauses before he spoke. They were meant to accomplish two things: 1) to fully understand what his interlocutor was saying and 2) to properly think out what he would say in response. He understood that words can have great power, but only if you take many things into account. You must be aware with whom you are speaking; what their emotional situation is; what their motivation for speaking is, etc. It appears that Yehudah was a master of communication, someone who fully appreciated the power of thought-out speech. Clearly, the effectiveness of his speech indicates that he carefully determined which words would have the most impact in each situation.

Also, in seeking the right timing, Yehudah shows his awareness of something the rabbis would later formalize: motivatory speech is only appropriate when it can work. The Talmud points out that it is just as much of a mitzvah not to give rebuke when it will not be accepted as it is to give rebuke when it will be accepted.[12] It is true that we can rarely be sure of the outcome of our efforts. Nevertheless, a leader has to keenly determine which outcome is more likely. Giving rebuke when it will be rebuffed is just as risky as failing to give it when it will be accepted; once a person has offered ineffective rebuke, it compromises their future effectiveness with that party.

Analyzing the leadership of Reuven and Yehudah helps us view communication in a more focused manner. We see the need to constantly be aware of how our speech will affect others. To do this we need to

---

[12] *Yevamot* 65b.

weigh our words carefully. We need to know what to say as well as when to say it.

Long before Dale Carneige ever came on the scene, the story of Reuven and Yehudah helps us understand what it takes to motivate people. Besides predating Carneige, the Torah conveys a crucial dimension missing from *How to Win Friends and Influence People* – the moral angle on good leadership. The message seems to be that it is Yehudah's respect for the dignity and opinions of others that allows him to get their support. We see this from his consistently understanding what others want and guiding their views accordingly. Thus, the Torah's narrative suggests that Yehudah's success is a natural result of a morally correct stance on leadership.

The Paradox of Jewish Leadership:
The House of Leah and the House of Rachel

Of the three candidates for leadership among Yaakov's sons, Yosef is the boldest and most flamboyant. On one level, Yosef has a legitimate birth-claim to the leadership. Since Rachel was meant to be Yaakov's first wife and Yosef was her firstborn, he could well have claimed to be Yaakov's natural heir. His claim seems further validated by his God-given good looks and abilities. Of the twelve brothers, it is only Yosef who could have become viceroy in Egypt. The other brothers simply didn't have the "right stuff." Yet in spite of Yosef's having all of the qualities we would expect in a leader, his bid for leadership is categorically rejected by his brothers. This rejection comes early on and is never truly reversed. Yaakov himself, at the end of his life, confirms the brothers' decision by reserving the leadership for Yehudah alone[13] – the lavish blessing given to Yosef and the double portion given to his children notwithstanding.

---

[13] *Bereshit* 49:10.

Yosef and the "Right Stuff"

To understand Yosef's rejection, we have to examine his political career more carefully. To begin with, we have to explain why Yosef was so determined to tell his dreams to his brothers. He certainly must have noticed the negative response the dreams always elicited. One possible reason is that Yosef wanted to inform his public of his aspirations. In typically political fashion, he must have felt that you can't win the race if you don't run. Thus, Yosef does what is usually necessary to attain leadership: he campaigns. In this vein, Yosef saw nothing wrong with publicizing the signs that confirmed his intuitive aspirations. After all, if leadership was his calling, this would benefit his entire family.

The text[14] gives us an additional hint to Yosef's early political behavior by mentioning a seemingly unimportant fact – that he would spend his time with the children of Bilhah. Rabbi Samson Raphael Hirsch provides us with a highly plausible explanation for this behavior. Could it not be that Yosef preferred to be with the children of maidservants, because they viewed themselves as his social inferiors? When he was with them, there was no contest for leadership and he could pursue his calling – without engendering the bitterness of Leah's children, who might have viewed their young brother's ambitions with suspicion.

To round out the picture, the Midrash tells us how Yosef would expend unusual effort on his personal grooming.[15] Given that such a view seems to fit the Biblical personality that emerges from the text, the Midrash may be revealing – as it is none other than a Jewish king that has a halachic obligation to cut his hair every day.[16] According to this, Yosef very early on seems to have felt the need to publicly prepare for his destiny by dressing the part of royalty.

---

[14] Ibid., 37:2.

[15] *Bereshit Rabba* 84:7.

[16] *Ta'anit* 17a.

Right Leader for the Wrong Nation

Yosef's father and brothers seem to view his political antics with a certain amount of disdain. His actions appear to grate against the fundamental spirit of Yaakov and his family. Thus, the brothers plot against Yosef because of his dreams of lording over his family and not because of the potentially more damaging tale bearing.[17] More than anything else then, it is Yosef's political behavior that eventually brings about his exile.

Ironically, it is in exile and among strangers where Yosef's politicking finds a more receptive response. In Egypt, Yosef becomes a tremendous success. In jail, he becomes even more popular than Aryeh Deri. In his charismatic way, he proceeds to make a monumental political comeback, reaching the highest office possible. In the world at large, he became the second most powerful man in the entire world – and on some level, the most powerful man.

However, Yosef's leadership in Egypt is typically functional – it is not the leadership of Jewish inspiration. Instead, it is the leadership of Noachide administration. Yosef's success is built on his ability to get things done, both as a campaigner and an administrator. In the Noachide world, this is all that is expected from a leader. But while positive in context, Yosef's style of leadership is not yet what it takes to become Yaakov's successor.

We get further insight into Yosef from an unusual source. An interesting point is made by Eliyahu Mizrachi and further developed in other later commentators.[18] Mizrachi asks a strong question concerning the rabbis' explanation of the "bad report" the Torah tells us Yosef gave about his brothers. According to the rabbis, one of the three things Yosef reported was that they ate flesh from a living animal, something forbidden even by Noachide law. Mizrachi questions the plausibility of Yosef's brothers straying so far from the path of their father. Based on

---

[17] *Bereshit* 37:19–20.

[18] See, for example, *Me'am Lo'ez*.

this question, later scholars come up with an ingenious approach to what may have transpired: The brothers were following Torah law, which allowed them to eat from an animal that was ritually slaughtered even though it was still moving, whereas Yosef held them accountable to Noachide law, which, in this case, was actually stricter.[19]

While this answer to Mizrachi's question is obviously speculative, it is no coincidence that Yosef is viewed as the defender of the Noachide code. In the Noachide world at large, a natural leader such as Yosef is expected to pursue leadership. It is equally not coincidental that the brothers insist on Torah law. Yosef's approach to leadership is foreign to the type of leader personality the Torah would later seek to create.

The idea of Yosef following a Noachide approach to leadership is further vindicated by an interesting phrase (*Bereshit* 42:7), wherein we are told that Yosef was "*yitnaker*" to his brothers. On the face of it, this means that he did not reveal his identity. Yet more than one commentator[20] understands the phrase to mean that Yosef was disguising himself by pretending to be a "*nochri*" (from the same Hebrew root as *yitnaker*), a non-Jew. Moreover, Yosef's dual identity is formalized by his being given an additional Egyptian name, something unparalleled in the foreign residence of any other personage in the Torah. From all of the above evidence, it appears that, on some level, Jewish tradition has long been aware of that which we are suggesting – that Yosef straddled the Jewish and Noachide worlds, whereas his brothers did not.

---

[19] This was at a time of lack of clarity about their status as halachic Jews. If, as the rabbis claim, the *Avot* were able to intuit Torah law (pre-dating the Sinai event), were they actually bound by it and not by Noachide law? The answer to this question is not clear.

[20] See, for example, Ibn Ezra and Rabbi S.R. Hirsch.

To Lead or Not to Lead

If there is indeed a Jewish approach to leadership that is distinct from the Noachide approach, it follows that the "right stuff" needed to be viceroy of Egypt was precisely what prevented Yosef from becoming the leader over his brothers and the Jewish people. In looking at classical Jewish leadership from Moshe to Gideon to Shaul to David, one finds a trait, common to them all, that is missing in Yosef. In all of the cases mentioned, the Jewish leader does not seek out leadership; on the contrary, he tries to avoid it. Such a tendency is most concretely expressed by *Midrash Tanchuma*,[21] explaining that a true Jewish leader is one who, like Shaul, runs away from leadership. This is not from lack of self-awareness, but from a realization of the ultimate distortion presented by human leadership. Even as we are commanded to imitate God in other ways, we need to be wary of imitating His trait of leadership. The Talmud points out the impropriety of being overly eager to accept even so seemingly innocuous a position as that of the *sheliach tzibur* (prayer leader).[22]

One problem with leadership is the need to decide what is right for others, something which only God Himself can truly know. A flesh and blood leader having to make such judgments blurs the distinction between man and God. Another problem with formalized human leadership is that it requires coercive power. On a mass level, leadership can only properly function when it has the power to force the recalcitrant. This is what is referred to as police powers or law enforcement. Endowing a man with these powers creates obvious difficulties. Since human justice cannot be perfect, the misuse of coercion that follows can have very undesirable consequences. This will occur in the best of situations, not to mention in instances wherein lesser states and individuals misuse power to their own advantage – the disastrous

---

[21] *Midrash Tanchuma* on *I Shmuel* 17:22.

[22] *Berachot* 34a.

results of which will often outweigh any benefits that coercion brings to a state in the first place.

Thus, the refined Jewish personality is hesitant to be put into a leadership situation, even while he or she must eventually accept it once it becomes clear that his or her leadership is needed. Even when required, it is not necessarily viewed as a permanent "position." Accordingly, ideal Jewish leadership is what was seen during the time of the Judges, wherein human leaders arose only to meet specific needs. When the need passed, those who were still alive went back to private life.[23] There are many who understand the Jewish desire for a formal leader during the days of Shmuel as moving away from this Jewish ideal.[24] Correspondingly, it was against this call for the power of office that Shmuel cried out so vigorously.

Proactive Self-Sacrifice

The Talmud compares the greatness of Yosef to that of Yehudah, stating that they both were able to make a *kiddush Hashem* (sanctification of God). At the same time, the Talmud states that Yehudah was greater. Whereas Yosef's *kiddush Hashem*, pushing off the advances of Potiphar's wife, was done in private, the Talmud points out that Yehudah's acknowledgment that he had mistreated Tamar occurred in public.[25] On the face of it, the comparison seems unfair. After all, Yosef's stand could have been taken only in private. Even as this is true, Yehudah's gesture did not have to be public. On the contrary, Tamar allowed for what we would expect any savvy politician to do – taking care of his debt to her

---

23 While this is not necessarily the case with all of the Judges, it is most clearly recorded concerning Gideon (*Shofetim* 8:23, 29) and appears to be depicted as the ideal in the parable of Yotam (ibid., 9:7–15).

24 Although this is not clear from the Biblical text.

25 *Sota* 10b (and 36b).

privately. Occasional scandals notwithstanding, this is inevitably the road of the Noachide politician. In Noachide politics, personal image is everything and consequently must be saved at all costs. Yehudah, however, as per the Talmud, is more interested in setting a personal example for his community than the resulting personal embarrassment. Thus, he went out of his way to make a private issue public, so that people could learn about the tremendous importance of honesty and accountability. In this, Yehudah is the prototype of a Jewish leader: completely focused on the content of his leadership, regardless of its personal political consequences.[26]

In the Jewish worldview, the person best qualified to take on a task does it without fanfare and without drawing attention to himself. On the contrary, while prepared to lead, the Jewish leader does not want to be thought of as a leader, a position with intrinsically problematic connotations. This was the case with Yehudah, who invited public disgrace in order to do what needed to be done. In marked contrast to Yosef, Yehudah showed little interest in his career as a leader. While the Talmud is not judging Yosef on missing an opportunity that wasn't granted to him, it does seem to identify the proactive self-sacrifice of Yehudah as a highly unusual trait that could only be found in a true Jewish leader such as he.

Yosef and Joe (Lieberman)

In comparing Yosef with Yehudah, we should not be too harsh in our treatment of the former. After all, Yosef was not only the viceroy of Egypt – he was also the defender and sustainer of the Jewish people in their first exile. It was Yosef who saved the Jewish people from famine,

---

[26] *Targum Yonatan* on *Bereshit* 49:8 makes this exact point by understanding Yaakov's blessing to Yehudah that his brothers will acknowledge him (as their leader) in the following manner: "Since you acknowledged the matter of Tamar, your brothers will acknowledge you…."

serving as an archetype of Jewish leadership in exile. Furthermore, the classical Jewish leadership of Yehudah will not be successful in exile. The truly Jewish politician who aims to provide moral leadership will encounter difficulty in the world at large (and it has been suggested that Yosef's modern namesake, Joe Lieberman, floundered in his bid for the American presidency for this very reason). It is only within the Jewish nation that such leadership will be sufficiently appreciated to work. In their exile, the Jewish people need Yosefs to protect them in their historical vulnerability.[27]

Yet just as Yehudah will not succeed in exile, Yosef will similarly not succeed in Israel. The disastrous consequences of applying the functional Noachide leadership model to Israel is clearly shown when Yosef's descendants attempt to reassert their ancestral claim to leadership. When Yeravam starts the northern kingdom of Israel, ripping away all the tribes from Yehudah (with the ironic exception of Yosef's brother Binyamin), it is a harbinger of one calamity after another.[28] The political judgment of Yeravam and his successors is based on the political considerations of the Noachide worldview. It is such considerations that move Yeravam to build an alternative to the Temple in his own territory. His decision to change the traditional calendar is also political in nature. While such an approach is doable in exile, it is a catastrophe for a Jewish state in Israel. As authoritatively discussed by Ramban,[29] Israel is a place where one has to live according to the ideal and not just the functional.

In summary, God gave the Jews two prototypical leaders – Yosef and Yehudah. Although the Jewish people need both, we look to Yehudah for our ideal. In seeking personal paradigms, even as we will

---

[27] It is interesting to note that Yosef's mother, Rachel, is also associated with exile. She dies shortly after entering Eretz Yisrael for the first time. Ramban explains that Yaakov could not remain married to two sisters in the more pristine spiritual atmosphere of Eretz Yisrael.

[28] *I Melachim*, Chaps. 12–14.

[29] Especially on *Vayikra* 18:25.

sometimes need to look to Yosef for guidance, we should always want to pursue the paradigm of Yehudah. Moreover, in recreating a Jewish state in Eretz Yisrael, we have to revert to the ideal. This is true in all realms, but especially in choosing our leaders. We cannot look to who will be pragmatically successful, as is the case for other states. Rather, we must seek true Jewish leaders, who will be completely willing to sacrifice themselves for the sake of the Jewish nation.

*   *   *

We have seen from the competition between Yehudah and Reuven that proper leadership of any type is rooted not only in skill, but also in the respect for and understanding of those whom one is leading. This is an important moral issue that the Torah wants to bring out. Although coercion may be a necessary evil for leading a large group, the primary approach of a successful leader will be to create consensus. Yehudah employs many important tools in order to bring about that consensus. He uses timing and communication skills, making sure he has the most likely chance of getting his interlocutors to weigh the merits of his vision. He also tries to place issues in the context of what is good for the entire group, making others more willing to listen. Finally, he remains goal-oriented, never losing sight of the big picture.

In our subsequent comparison of Yehudah and Yosef, we have seen that being a capable and moral leader is not enough to make one into a *Jewish* leader. As opposed to Yosef, Yehudah is the quintessential Jewish leader, whose focus on the national interest is completely divorced from personal advancement. Even more crucial, an archetypal Jewish leader like Yehudah cannot help but be uneasy with the notion of leadership altogether, as leadership is ultimately appropriate only for God Himself.

In spite of Yehudah's appropriate hesitations, he is literally obligated to show leadership when the need arises. What is true of

Yehudah is true of each one of us. The Jewish concept of *arevut* (mutual responsibility) requires that we worry about not only our own growth and progress, but also that of others as well. Inasmuch as leadership is a calling for all Jews – at least as parents, but usually even beyond that, as a "nation of priests" – it is fitting to take a close look at the do's and don'ts of Yehudah, Yosef and Reuven.

Redeeming Relevance

Creativity and Rigor

It is my hope that these essays have been successful *parshanut* (commentary). I have attempted to write them within the dynamic that traditionally marks successful Jewish commentaries.

When teaching, I often mention my belief that Jewish genius expresses itself exclusively by working within the tension between intellectual rigor on the one side and individual creativity on the other. That is to say, an important Jewish work must tap into the creative juices of the author while still conforming to the demands that result from respecting the integrity of the text. This may be the key to the greatness of Jewish writings: the author's ability to create beautiful innovative worlds, while still keeping both feet planted firmly on the ground.

It is obvious that a commentary that lacks creativity will rarely interest us. Such a commentary will only be telling us something that we could see from the text itself, that has already become well-known in another context or that does not contain anything that captures our imaginations. At the same time, however, commentary that lacks rigor is no longer text-based and becomes completely the thoughts of the author. No matter how interesting these thoughts are, they can no longer claim to be legitimate commentary as traditionally understood. Thus, whether consciously or not, the commentator must constantly check himself with these two yardsticks, asking the dual questions of "Is this true?" and "Is this interesting?"

The nature of the storyteller is to embellish the story in order to make it more interesting. Like any author, the commentator is also likely to be tempted by the potential reaction of the reader to say more than that for which there is good evidence. Having found something to be true, it is sometimes difficult to know where to stop. At what point does analysis become conjecture? At what point is that conjecture still legitimate, and at what point does it become fanciful? One must constantly keep these questions in mind and not overstate his reading of the holy text.

Creativity cannot be allowed to overshadow the integrity of the Biblical text. Nechama Leibowitz writes that "the primary demand of *parshanut* is that it responds to the spirit, tone and intention of the narrative."[1] I would add that good commentaries must deal with language, nuance, plot and other literary issues in a convincing manner. In other words, if the text says black, no matter how badly a commentator would like to say white, he cannot. Even while the Torah's message is refracted through the mind and culture of the human interpreter, parameters of legitimacy such as the ones mentioned above create necessary restrictions to individual creativity. As such, adherence to these parameters constitutes a traditional *sine qua non* to a commentary's validity as commentary. Failure to live up to these standards is failure to convince the reader that the idea is rooted in the text. In traditional Judaism, this rootedness is critical.

Yet we should not dismiss an author's desire to interest his reader as a purely base motive for writing. The desire to say something new and interesting serves to motivate him to explore possibilities that would otherwise go unexplored. Ideas that may be very valid would sometimes

---

[1] Nechama Leibowitz, *Studies in Bereshit*, p. 366 (*Vayishlach* 4).

never see the light of day due to the overbearing concern not to make mistakes.

In this regard, the author's drive to interest his readers may be compared to the rabbis' understanding of what they call the *yetzer ha-ra*. Literally translated as the impulse to do evil, a more nuanced translation would understand the *yetzer ha-ra* as the motivation to advance our selfish good. The Talmud speaks about the complete cessation of world activities that would result from the elimination of such motivation.[2] In our case as well, the author's "selfish" drives push him to greater creativity that will make for a better work. Thus, it is entirely appropriate for the commentator to seek that which is novel and significant. If not, he will ultimately write things that are trite and of little consequence.

God's Voice in History

Of course, the notion of rootedness mentioned above is not just important as a means through which to convince readers of the author's ideas, but rather it is important in and of itself: The idea of Torah commentary is the search to understand God's word. Thus, a more critical reason for the vital set of checks and balances is to force us to root our own thought in the Divine will.

In reflecting the Divine voice, *parshanut* serves a critical function: In post-Biblical times, it may well be the closest thing we have to the Divine voice itself. All historical Jewish communities have their own specific issues that need to be addressed by the Divine voice. By the finite nature of its words, however, the Torah cannot, and perhaps does not want to, explicitly address every individual Jewish culture. Throughout most of Jewish history, it has been the role of the Torah commentators to try to understand the Torah's implications for their own times. Indeed,

---

[2] *Yoma* 69b.

consciously or not, Torah commentators throughout the generations have discussed novel ideas they found implicit in the Torah and that spoke to their own cultural contexts.

Parshanut has thus allowed the Torah's terse writing on the one hand, and its myriad implications on the other, to provide a framework within which to judge ourselves and to chart a course for the future. This open-ended dynamic has provided the Jewish people with the ability to connect with the Divine will throughout the long march of history. Our commentators can only reflect the Divine voice, however, as long as they respect the holy integrity of the text.

In this context, it is important to understand the difference between *parshanut* and prophecy. In *parshanut*, there is much more room for variation. The Divine voice in the text is often not monolithic, so that the text may actually broadcast two contradictory messages even to the same historical period. As a result, *parshanut* is not meant to give clear instruction in the same way as prophecy. Indeed, the confusion created by such a lack of absolute direction is a most intended characteristic of the cessation of prophecy. Nevertheless, even if we are not to get unqualified direction, we can still get guidance as to what are the appropriate and inappropriate values operative in any given society.

Thus, if there has been a serious decline in *parshanut*, it is no trivial matter. It is tantamount to cutting off the Divine voice in our times. More precisely, it is an abdication of our responsibility to listen to that voice and hear what it is saying *specifically to us*. Of all times for such a trend to occur, it is ironic that precisely in our day when there are so many unprecedented changes, we would lose the ability or desire to seek direction in contemporary Torah commentary. I cannot think of a more critical time than our own to seek the Divine guidance waiting to be revealed via proper novel readings of the Torah.

Parshanut Today and Tomorrow

It must be noted that in recent years, there has been a resurgence of traditional interpretation of the Torah. In Hebrew, Rabbi Yoel ben Nun, among others, has worked tirelessly to seek out a contemporary understanding of the text which appropriately incorporates scholarly research of ancient Near-East cultures. In English, Dr. Avivah Gottlieb Zornberg has applied contemporary psychological and literary insights in her novel exegetical work on the text. There are many others who have also recently taken a more systematic and sophisticated approach in this field.

The question that must be raised concerning contemporary work in *parshanut* is whether it will prove itself to be really great in historical terms. In other words, whether any of the recent works on the Torah will stand the test of time remains to be seen. It is still too early to know whether recent efforts at creating something of lasting value to Jewish society have been successful.

Perhaps, as some believe, people writing in this field nowadays are incapable of producing something truly great. On a personal level, I am constantly haunted by this possibility. I do not know if I will ever be able to produce something of lasting value in the field. On the contrary, I know how far I am from the great commentators of yesteryear. For this reason, I think of Nechama Leibowitz's warning to those who are not "truly great," not to waste their time writing things very few people will read.[3] Such concerns need be taken seriously and cannot but engender hesitation.

---

[3] From a letter to R. Netanel Helfgot published in *Pirkei Nechama*, p. 662. It is interesting to note that, due to her great modesty, Nechama herself rarely entered into the world of commentary *per se*. Nechama's works are full of others' ideas, which she dissects and evaluates with great aplomb, but as for new and original ideas on the meaning of the text, she refrained.

That being said, I can only work with my intuition which points me in the direction of Chazal's dictate, "In a place where there are no men, attempt to be a man."[4] By this I do not mean that there are no other individuals working seriously in the field of *parshanut*, but rather that *all* such individuals must do whatever they can to bring back the Divine voice to our people. It is in this spirit that I have been motivated to present the fruits of my labors, hoping that it will somehow contribute to regaining the Divine voice. If nothing else, perhaps the mere attempt at creating something of value in this vital field will serve as a model and inspiration for others who are more able to take up this task, so critical to the future of the Jewish people.

If we are able, we must strive to put out works of tremendous quality. Scholars must expand their horizons and, by putting forth their best efforts, engender the resulting demand for their original work. But it is not only up to scholars to create the demand by putting out works of obvious value – it is also up to the learned public to encourage and challenge their teachers by seeking the best that can be produced. They can do this by expecting creativity, relevance and rigor – and by settling for nothing less.

---

[4] *Avot* 2:5.

About the Author

Rabbi Francis Nataf is Educational Director of the David Cardozo Academy and has previously held senior educational positions in Israel and the United States. Rabbi Nataf was ordained at Yeshiva University and also holds degrees in Jewish history and international affairs. He has published numerous articles on Jewish thought and education.

Publication of this book was assisted by the
The David Cardozo Academy
Machon Ohr Aaron
7 Cassuto Street
Jerusalem 96433 Israel
Tel: 972 2 652 4053 Fax: 972 2 654 2072
Email: cacademy@012.net.il
www.cardozoschool.org